NOTES

Display Your Work! Get Noticed! Why Ask Why? Ask Why Not?!

In most states and most counties across America, a fair is held each summer. And each of these fairs solicits various art, crafts and writing pieces from kids for judging and display at the fair. Consider applying this year by submitting one of your crafts or creative writing pieces and you could earn ribbons, awards and sometimes even cash prizes! PS – Don't wait until the fair to take action! While fairs will only want your actual work dropped off 6-8 weeks (at most) before the fair, most fairs require you to submit an easy application 2-4 months before the fair! Look on fair websites for details on how to apply.

More often than not, teachers, students and parents are asked to raise funds for their schools. And the business minded kids are always looking to find a way to earn some cash for their piggy banks or their favorite local charities. Consider using recycled containers to grow seeds and sell mature seedlings or full-grown plants for $2-$5 each to earn some cash. It's a great way to make money while recycling and providing people with plants that can feed them over and over again!

WHAT'S ON THE BACK OF LESSON PAGES? Creative Writing & Plant Data

Each lesson provides you with a creative writing prompt to help you start your story. Use the space on the back of each lesson's page to write your story. Use more paper if needed.

There is also space to sketch and record data for two different plants you are growing (don't choose the same type of plant). You should sketch and record data for the same two plants each week. There are several reasons to record data about your plants, such as finding the ones that grow well and produce the most amount of food in your climate. Measuring plant growth and counting leaves are two types of data that take just a little time to collect and record each week. There is also space to circle any leaf or plant observations from week to week such as the discoloration of leaves or the presence of flowers or fruit on the plant.

FIRST, fill in some basic information about the two plants you have selected to sketch and measure data on. You may need to look at a calendar and your seed packets for some information. You will need this information to perform your weekly calculations.

Plant #1:

Plant #2:

Date Seeds Planted Indoors:

Date Seeds Planted Indoors:

Total Expected Days To Harvest:

Total Expected Days To Harvest:

Sketches

Sketch your two plants carefully in the illustrated pots provided. Use colored pencils to add color and details. Try to sketch the plants with the same proportion (size) and from the same perspective (viewed from a particular point) each time. For example, look at your plant's cup with your name marked on the front and draw from that perspective each time. If your plant was 1mm tall one week and 1.5mm the next week, don't draw a plant as short as a marble one week and as tall as a tree the next week – you would first draw a plant the same size as the plant drawn in the previous week, and only add half of that height to the plant the current week. Keep the plant in proportion from week to week!

Days To Harvest

To calculate when to expect food from your plants (*Days Until Harvest*), subtract the number of days since you started the seeds from the *Total Expected Days To Harvest* (see above). You may need a calendar to help you with this calculation.

Growth Increase

Measure each of your selected plants as it grows from week to week by placing a ruler (or measuring tape when it grows beyond a ruler's height!) at the base of the plant and measuring to the tip. It is best to measure the growth in millimeters (mm).

1 millimeter | 10 millimeters

```
|||||||||||||||||||||||||||||||||||||||||
0   1   2   3   4   5   6   7   8   9  10  11  12
mm
```

REMEMBER TO PLOT YOUR DATA
ON THE GRAPH ON THE BACK OF THIS PAGE

EXAMPLE:
WEEKLY SKETCHES
AND PLANT HEIGHT
MEASUREMENTS

| 0mm | 1mm | 10mm | 20mm |
| WEEK 1 | 2 | 3 | 4 |

To calculate how much your plant has grown from the previous week, subtract last week's measurement from the current week's measurement and record that data next to *Growth Increase* for each plant.

% Increase

To calculate the percentage of growth increase from the previous week, first find the difference (*Growth Increase*) between last week and this week's plant height. Then divide the increase (*Growth Increase*) by the original number (last week's measurement) and multiply the answer by 100.

For example:
If a plant measured 4mm in height last week, and 6mm this week:

$$\frac{6 - 4}{4} = \frac{2}{4} = 0.5$$

$0.5 \times 100 = 50\%$
growth increase from last week

PLANT GROWTH OVER TIME

PLANT: PLANT:

HEIGHT IN MILLIMETERS

460
440
420
400
380
360
340
320
300
280
260
240
220
200
180
160
140
120
100
80
60
40
20

1 2 3 4 5 6 7 8 9 10 11 12 13 14 15 16 17 18 19 20 21 22 23 24 25 26 27 28 29 30 31 32

WEEK

MY GARDEN PLAN

	Spacing Between Seeds	Plant In Full Sun	Plant In Partial Sun	Seed Planting Depth	Days To Germinate	Days To Harvest	Thin Seedlings	Water Requirements	Container Size	Growing Season	JAN	FEB	MAR	APR	MAY	JUN	JUL	AUG	SEP	OCT	NOV	DEC
Cucumbers	3"	Y		1/2"	7	45	Y	D	M	SP S												

JUST FOR FUN GARDEN COLORING PAGE

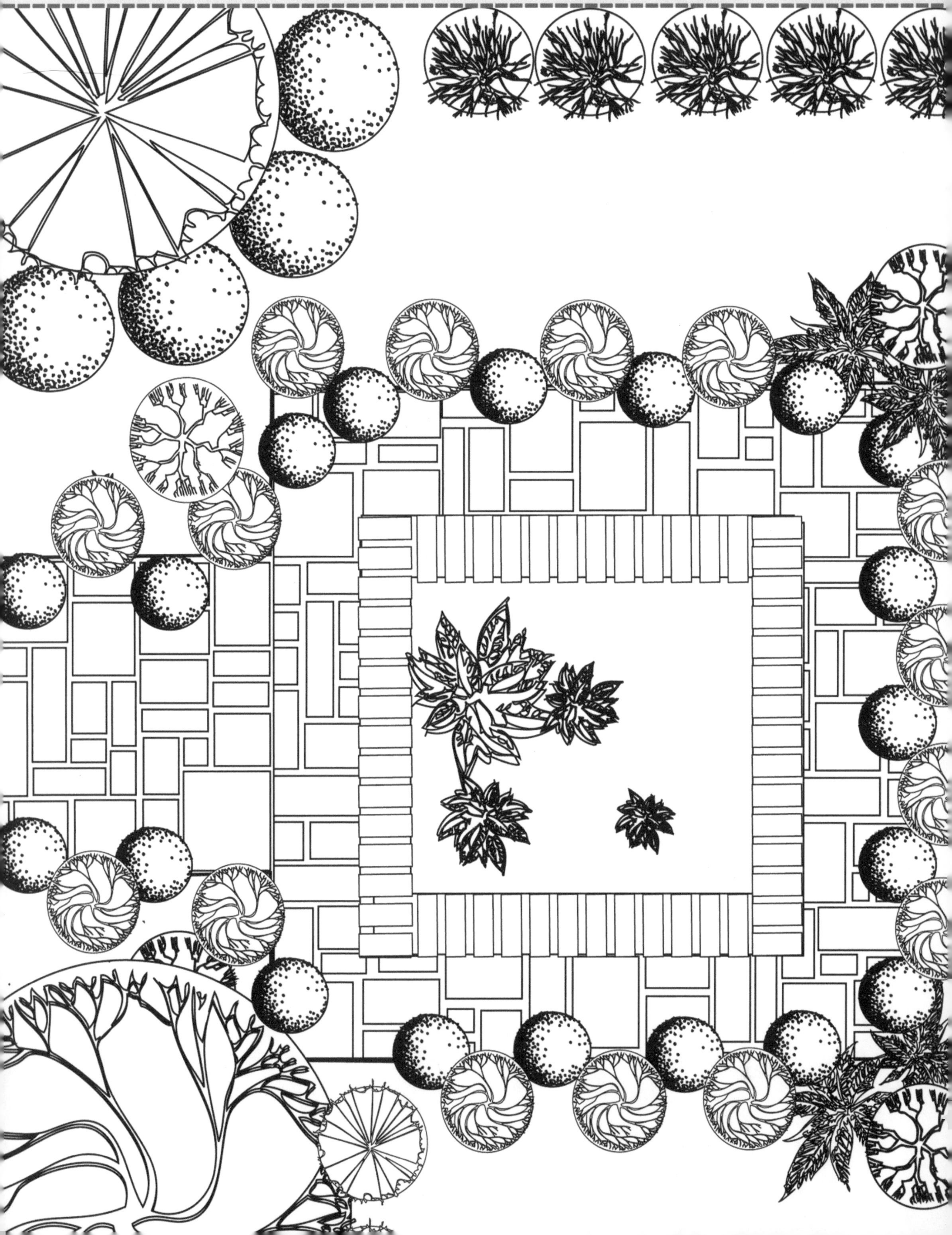

Lesson 1

CLIMATE (noun):
the weather conditions of a particular area, including temperature, rain, sunshine, cloudiness, and winds, throughout the year

PROJECT:
PERSONAL GARDEN PLANNING

FOOD
FOR YOUR BRAIN

The walnut tree in Martha's backyard is 54 years old and the walnut tree at her mother's house is 80 years old.

How many years ago was Martha's mother's tree three times the age of her tree?

Having a garden that always provides food for you is an ongoing, year round project. Initial planning can save you disappointment, time, money and energy. By following these basic guidelines, your garden will be off to a flying start and will give you pleasure and satisfaction year round.

What should I plant?
1. Know what you like to eat most! There is no point in planting beets if you won't eat them! Save your garden space for what you enjoy and will use.

2. Where do you live? There are many guides in books and online that will let you know the best vegetables to plant in your area, based on your <u>climate</u>, which is a great help when deciding what to plant in your garden. Find seeds that will germinate and grow in your climate. Each seed packet lists climate, water, plant spacing, and soil requirements as well as expected germination and harvest (the total time to produce mature fruits and vegetables that you can eat!) time and estimated plant heights.

Where should I put my garden?
Where does the sun strike your garden, and for how long? Make sure your vegetable garden gets at least 5 hours a day of direct sunlight, although places with less sun can provide enough sun for certain leafy vegetables and herbs. And make sure your taller plants won't block the sunlight for the shorter plants.

When should I plant my garden?
Almost anytime of year is a good time of year to plant your garden! In cooler fall and winter months, plants like broccoli, brussels sprouts, cauliflower, turnips, and cabbage grow best. In warmer months, they simply may not grow. In warmer spring and summer months, plants like corn, tomato, eggplant, squash and melons grow best. If you try to plant these in cooler months, they may just curl up their toes and die.

BOOKS
Climate Maps
by Ian F. Mahaney

Growing California Native Plants
by Marjorie Schmidt

Sunset Western
Garden Book

CREATIVE
WRITING PROMPT
Pick a seed packet. What kind of plant will your seed grow into? What climate do you grow in? What are your planting requirements? Will you have flowers? Will you grow food?

CREATIVE WRITING

GERMINATION (verb):
the process by which a plant grows from a seed

PROJECT:
STARTING SEEDS

FOOD
FOR YOUR BRAIN

Can you place six sunflower seeds on a Tic Tac Toe board without making three-in-a-row in any direction?

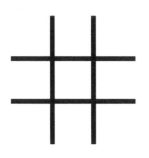

Starting seed indoors is the best way to get your garden off to an early start as seeds are hard to keep track of outdoors and are too easily washed away or eaten by pests when very young. When you start your seeds indoors, you can control conditions such as heat, light, and moisture, yielding larger plants that are better able to thrive and produce more food once moved outdoors.

There are a number of factors that affect seed germination:
1. Soil Temperature - If the soil is too cold the seeds can rot

2. Soil Moisture - If the soil is too wet, the seeds will be swollen, soft, and rotten. If the soil is too dry, the seeds will dry out.

3. Age of Seeds - If the seeds are too old, they may no longer be viable.

4. Seed Depth When Planting - Some seeds need more or less light when planted and if seeds are planted too deeply, they may not sprout. Seed size usually is a good indication of how deep to plant your seeds, which usually corresponds to how much light they need. The general rule of thumb is to plant your seeds at least as deep as the seed is long.

If one or more of these factors are not ideal for a particular type of plant, the germination process will stop and plants won't have their roots take hold to grow into a successful, living plant.

> **Viable**
> (adjective):
> capable of working successfully

CREATIVE
WRITING PROMPT

You found a tiny tomato seed. Write a letter to the tomato seed to tell it why it needs to be planted and grow into a plant.

BOOKS

How a Seed Grows
by Helene J. Jordan

Starting Seeds: How to Grow Healthy, Productive Vegetables, Herbs, and Flowers from Seed
by Barbara Ellis

CREATIVE WRITING & PLANT NOTES

Plant:

Days Until Harvest:

Leaves:

Plant Height:

Growth Increase:

% Increase:

Are any leaves:

discolored   eaten   dry broken

Is the plant:

dead   rotten   flowering   fruiting

Plant:

Days Until Harvest:

Leaves:

Plant Height:

Growth Increase:

% Increase:

Are any leaves:

discolored   eaten   dry broken

Is the plant:

dead   rotten   flowering   fruiting

CONTAINER (noun):
an object that can be used to hold or transport something

PROJECT:
BURLAP & PAINT PLANTER COVERS

FOOD
FOR YOUR BRAIN

All of my flowers except two are roses. All of my flowers except two are tulips. All of my flowers except two are daisies.

How many flowers do I have?

Container gardening allows you to maximize small spaces while still growing all the herbs, flowers and produce that you need. Almost any plant can grow well either indoors or outdoors in containers as long as they have plenty of sun and water.

By simply poking a few drainage holes on the bottom of any container, you can turn almost anything into a suitable container for growing plants. Everything from bowls to barrels to milk jugs or cartons can be used as a container for growing plants.

In larger 3-5 gallon pots you can grow beans, carrots, peppers, tomatoes, corn, broccoli, cabbage, kale, leeks and melons.

Medium size pots work well for beets, eggplant and cherry tomatoes.

Pots as small as 4-6 inches are great for growing peas, lettuce, spinach and Swiss chard.

And any size container will work well for fresh herbs!

CREATIVE
WRITING PROMPT

You are an herb garden planted in a lovely blue pot, sitting on the balcony of a New York City apartment building. Describe your life. Who picks the herbs, how often are they picked, and how do they get used?

BOOKS

Kids Container Gardening:
Year-Round Projects
for Inside and Out
by Cindy Krezel

A Kid's Guide to
Container Gardening
by Stephanie Bearce

Plant:

Days Until Harvest:

Leaves:

Plant Height:

Growth Increase:

% Increase:

Are any leaves:

discolored   eaten   dry   broken

Is the plant:

dead   rotten   flowering   fruiting

Plant:

Days Until Harvest:

Leaves:

Plant Height:

Growth Increase:

% Increase:

Are any leaves:

discolored   eaten   dry   broken

Is the plant:

dead   rotten   flowering   fruiting

Lesson 4

REGENERATION (noun):
the regrowth by an animal or plant of
a part that has been lost or destroyed

PROJECT:
PAINT STICK PLANT MARKERS

FOOD
FOR THE BRAIN

If a girl and a half could eat a pineapple and a half in a minute and a half, how many pineapples could six girls eat in six minutes?

Many fruit and vegetable scraps can be directly regrown into new food that is organic, edible, tasty, healthy and nutritious. And the cycle of growing new food from scraps is a quicker alternative to growing plants from seeds that can be repeated over and over again, allowing you to produce an unending supply of fruits and vegetables from food scraps that you ordinarily might have composted or thrown away. What a great way to recycle!

There are dozens of fruits and vegetables that can be easily regrown including:

Green Onions & Leeks - Green onions and leeks can quickly be _regenerated_ by simply sticking their root ends in a glass of water. Place the glass in sunlight and change the water every couple of days.

Celery & Lettuce - Put the root end in a glass of water and watch it grow back. In about a week, it will be ready for planting. And in just 3-4 weeks after that, you'll have a whole new head of celery or lettuce ready to eat.

Pineapple - To regrow pineapples, you simply need to remove the crown, the green leafy piece at the top, and plant your pineapple crown in a warm place with good moist soil.

Potatoes & Sweet Potatoes - When you see one of your potatoes or sweet potatoes growing "eyes," cut it into one inch pieces, leaving 2 eyes per piece. Let the cut pieces sit out for a few days, allowing it to dry out a bit. Plant the pieces 6-8 inches deep in soil and watch each piece grow into lots of new potatoes in about 3 months!

CREATIVE
WRITING PROMPT

You are writing a book called _Trash To Treasure_. The book is about regenerating food that would normally be trash taking up space in our landfills. Write the first page of the book.

BOOKS

Don't Throw It, Grow It!:
68 Windowsill Plants
From Kitchen Scraps
by Deborah Peterson

Food Scrap Gardening: How To
Grow Food from Scraps, Reduce
Waste and Feed the World
by Will Cook

Plant:

Days Until Harvest:

Leaves:

Plant Height:

Growth Increase:

% Increase:

Are any leaves:

discolored   eaten   dry broken

Is the plant:

dead   rotten   flowering   fruiting

Plant:

Days Until Harvest:

Leaves:

Plant Height:

Growth Increase:

% Increase:

Are any leaves:

discolored   eaten   dry broken

Is the plant:

dead   rotten   flowering   fruiting

Lesson 5

WEAR AND TEAR (noun):
damage, depreciation, or loss resulting from ordinary use

PROJECT:
PLANT SEEDLINGS IN OUTSIDE CONTAINERS

FOOD
FOR THE BRAIN

You have a jug that holds five gallons, and a jug that holds three gallons. You have no other containers, and there are no markings on the jugs. You need to obtain exactly seven gallons of water from a faucet to water the new tree in the garden. How can you do it?

All gardens require maintenance. Weather, weeds, and <u>wear and tear</u> all take their toll on both plants and the garden they're planted in.

Ensure your fruits, veggies and flowers thrive by following this simple basic guideline for maintaining your garden:

1. Water seeds and plants daily or weekly depending on the watering requirements of each plant. Vegetables need water to grow and lots of it. Do NOT let your seeds or garden bed dry out!

2. Clean up any trash or fallen debris in the yard around the garden

3. Pull weeds in pots

4. Remove leaves and dead foliage from in and around pots and the garden

5. Cut dead or damaged leaves, stems and flowers

CREATIVE
WRITING PROMPT

Miss Wicked Weed has found your garden and she plans on taking over. Finish this story.

BOOKS

How a Seed Grows
by Helene J. Jordan

How Does a Seed Sprout?
by Melissa Stewart

Starting Seeds
by Barbara Ellis

CREATIVE WRITING & PLANT NOTES

Plant:

Days Until Harvest:

Leaves:

Plant Height:

Growth Increase:

% Increase:

Are any leaves:

discolored eaten dry broken

Is the plant:

dead rotten flowering fruiting

Plant:

Days Until Harvest:

Leaves:

Plant Height:

Growth Increase:

% Increase:

Are any leaves:

discolored eaten dry broken

Is the plant:

dead rotten flowering fruiting

BENEFIT (noun):
something that produces a good or helpful result

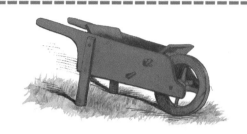

PROJECT:
TOILET PAPER ROLL SEEDLING GIFTS

FOOD
FOR THE BRAIN

You have managed to squeeze two cups of juice from the citrus fruits grown in your yard, one containing orange juice and one containing and equal amount of lemonade. One teaspoon of the orange juice is taken and mixed with the lemonade. Then a teaspoon of this mixture is mixed back into the orange juice. Is there more lemonade in the orange juice or more orange juice in the lemonade?

There are many <u>benefits</u> to growing food in your own garden:

1. Better Diet: Growing your own food helps you eat more fresh fruits and vegetables without using harmful poisons that are necessary for producing the masses of produce you see in grocery stores.

2. More Flavor & Nutrition: Since many store bought fruits and vegetables must be picked early, they lose flavor and nutrients. So when fruits and vegetables can ripen in your own garden and are picked fresh, they have more flavor and more nutrients.

3. More Exercise & Fresh Air: You get more physical activity and fresh air by getting outside and moving around in your garden. Planting, weeding, watering, and harvesting all add purposeful physical activity to your day.

4. Help The Environment: When you add vegetable trimmings, eggshells, coffee grounds, and tea bags to your compost bin, which in turn goes back into the soil in your garden, you help nourish the delicious food you are growing and throw less in the trash cans to go into the landfills. You'll also reduce the use of fossil fuels and the resulting pollution that comes from the transport of fresh produce from all over the world in planes and refrigerated trucks to your grocery store.

5. Save Money: Fresh fruits and vegetables are expensive when you buy them at grocery stores and farmer's markets. Growing your own fruits and vegetables, including using regrowth methods, and harvesting seeds, can really save you and your family money while producing delicious food at the same time.

6. Connection, Appreciation & Pride: When you grow your own food, you have more pride in yourself because you know the effort and patience it took to produce your own food. It also allows you to take time to reflect on how fortunate we are to have fresh food to eat. And we can appreciate the opportunity to connect with our families, friends and classmates by sharing our food and eating together

CREATIVE
WRITING PROMPT

A plant is dying.
Tell it why it needs to live.

BOOKS

Ready, Set, Grow!
A Kid's Guide
to Gardening
by Rebecca Spohn

CREATIVE WRITING & PLANT NOTES

Plant:

Days Until Harvest:

Leaves:

Plant Height:

Growth Increase:

% Increase:

Are any leaves:

discolored   eaten   dry broken

Is the plant:

dead   rotten   flowering   fruiting

Plant:

Days Until Harvest:

Leaves:

Plant Height:

Growth Increase:

% Increase:

Are any leaves:

discolored   eaten   dry broken

Is the plant:

dead   rotten   flowering   fruiting

ACCIDENT (noun): any event that happens unexpectedly usually resulting in harm, injury, damage, or loss

PROJECT:
MINI GARDEN SAFETY SIGNS

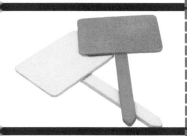

FOOD
FOR THE BRAIN

The school garden shed contains ten pairs of blue gardening gloves and ten pairs of gray gardening gloves. If you're only allowed to take one glove from the gloves drawer at a time and you can't see what color glove you're taking until you've taken it, how many gloves do you have to take before you're guaranteed to have at least one matching pair?

Safety in the garden is something we all cannot take seriously enough.

While we all know that accidents happen (that's why they are called accidents!), following some basic garden safety rules can prevent the majority of <u>accidents</u>. And although most of these garden safety rules are common sense, it never hurts to be reminded of them:

1. Gardening tools are tools and not toys. Waving tools around or pretending to cut somebody or something with any tool is not smart.

2. Don't eat anything without asking an adult first - there are a number of poisonous plants, berries and flowers that look delicious and can seriously harm or kill you if eaten and swallowed.

3. Wear gloves when handling wood, thorny plants, and spiky plants to avoid splinters and cuts.

4. Do not pick up garden bugs or animals as they may bite

5. Don't put your hands in places you can't see! Spiders, snakes, bees and other creatures like to hide in and around gardens, so always look where you put your hands and feet before you put them there!

6. Wear sunscreen, a hat and a lightweight long sleeved shirt if working outside in the sun for a long period of time. And always wear closed toe shoes to prevent any injuries to your sweet feet!

7. Drink lots of water to stay hydrated when working outside in your garden.

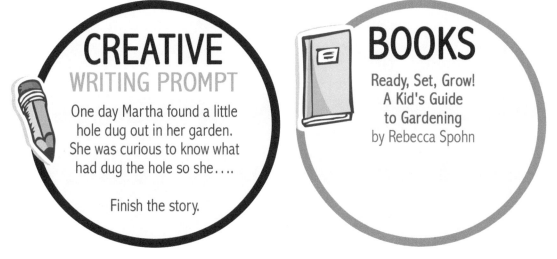

CREATIVE
WRITING PROMPT

One day Martha found a little hole dug out in her garden. She was curious to know what had dug the hole so she....

Finish the story.

BOOKS

Ready, Set, Grow!
A Kid's Guide
to Gardening
by Rebecca Spohn

Plant:

Days Until Harvest:

Leaves:

Plant Height:

Growth Increase:

% Increase:

Are any leaves:

discolored eaten dry broken

Is the plant:

dead rotten flowering fruiting

Plant:

Days Until Harvest:

Leaves:

Plant Height:

Growth Increase:

% Increase:

Are any leaves:

discolored eaten dry broken

Is the plant:

dead rotten flowering fruiting

TOOL(noun):
anything used as a means of accomplishing a task or purpose

PROJECT:
SHRINKY DINK GARDEN MAGNETS

FOOD
FOR YOUR BRAIN

A certain five letter word becomes shorter when you add two letters to it.

What is the word?

Garden <u>tools</u> come in all shapes, sizes and vary in the ways we can use them.

Some popular garden tools for smaller container gardens can include:

1. Garden Spade - a great tool for turning the soil, aerating, and mixing compost and nutrients into the soil.

2. Trowel - a small handheld tool with either a curved scoop or a flat, pointed blade for lifting plants or soil

3. Hori Hori Knife - this is an "all purpose" garden tool that is great for digging, weeding, planting, cutting bags open and so many more things!

4. Pruning Shears - your plants may or may not need some pruning, but if they do, pruning shears are a great cutting tool good for cutting unwanted greenery or for cutting vegetables and fruits off a plant when it's harvest time

5. Watering Can - while any container will do, a watering can with small holes of the same size can distribute the water evenly and gentler, especially for young seeds and seedlings. Milk jugs with holes poked in the cap make great watering cans.

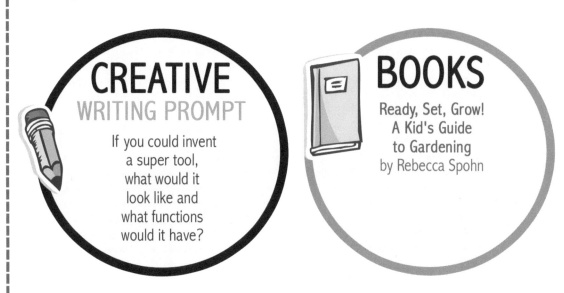

CREATIVE
WRITING PROMPT
If you could invent a super tool, what would it look like and what functions would it have?

BOOKS
Ready, Set, Grow!
A Kid's Guide
to Gardening
by Rebecca Spohn

Plant:

Days Until Harvest:

Leaves:

Plant Height:

Growth Increase:

% Increase:

Are any leaves:

discolored   eaten   dry   broken

Is the plant:

dead   rotten   flowering   fruiting

Plant:

Days Until Harvest:

Leaves:

Plant Height:

Growth Increase:

% Increase:

Are any leaves:

discolored   eaten   dry   broken

Is the plant:

dead   rotten   flowering   fruiting

SOIL (noun):
the upper layer of earth in which plants grow, consisting of rock and mineral particles mixed with decayed organic matter

PROJECT:
LEAF ART CARDS

FOOD
FOR YOUR BRAIN

A girl had nine perfect, dry leaves, and all but seven crumbled.

How many perfect, dry leaves did she have left?

Healthy soil:

• Holds moisture, but drains well: plants need water, but not too much or too little

• Has plenty of vitamins and minerals: vitamins and minerals are essential for vigorous plant growth

• Is loose and fluffy filled with air: plants need air, both above ground and in the soil

Plant roots have a hard time growing in sandy soil because water quickly drains through and cannot be used by the plant roots.

Plant roots have a hard time growing in hard clay soil because the soil gets waterlogged and filled with water, drowning plant roots.

Mulch is any type of material that is laid over the surface of the soil as a covering. Organic materials like wood chips and leaves are best because they eventually decompose and add nutrients to the soil. Other common materials used for mulch are stone or gravel, straw, compost and newspaper.

Benefits of mulch in your garden:

• Keeps weeds under control by reducing sunlight to weed seeds

• Regulates soil temperature, cooling it in summer and insulating it in winter

• Conserves moisture; mulch can mean life or death for plants during drought

• Improves the appearance of a garden

• Creates habitat for beneficial organisms such as earthworms

CREATIVE
WRITING PROMPT

Write a story titled *I Love You Very Mulch* that has the characters King Soil and Queen Mulch.

BOOKS

Life in a Bucket of Soil
by Alvin Silverstein

Dirt: The Scoop on Soil
by Natalie M. Rosinsky

Look What I Did with a Leaf!
by Morteza E. Sohi

CREATIVE WRITING & PLANT NOTES

Plant:

Days Until Harvest:

Leaves:

Plant Height:

Growth Increase:

% Increase:

Are any leaves:

discolored eaten dry broken

Is the plant:

dead rotten flowering fruiting

Plant:

Days Until Harvest:

Leaves:

Plant Height:

Growth Increase:

% Increase:

Are any leaves:

discolored eaten dry broken

Is the plant:

dead rotten flowering fruiting

Lesson 10

MICRO-ORGANISMS (noun):
the smallest of the small and the simplest of the simple living things that can only be seen with a microscope

PROJECT:
COMPOST COLLECTION+
AWARENESS POSTERS

FOOD
FOR THE BRAIN

A family of worms is enjoying their carefree life in your compost bin abounding with delicious food. They have built many tunnels in the compost pile. The entrance to their main tunnel is a hole that is two millimeters wide, three millimeters long, and four millimeters deep. How much dirt is there in the hole?

Bacteria and fungi are <u>micro-organisms</u> that feed on the waste, breaking it down into hot compost - they either come in naturally from the soil or they are added in as a sprinkling of fresh soil every so often. All dead plants and organic waste will rot down and decompose if you leave them alone, turning into a soil-like material called compost. Composting is a natural way of recycling!

Compost Recipe

> Compost and soil are not dead, they are living things!

✔ 1 part green plant waste (dead plants, leaves, flowers and grass cuttings)

✔ 1 part brown plant waste (bark, roots, twigs)

> **Bad Composting Ingredients:**
> Meat, bones, whole eggs, dairy products
> (cheese, milk, yogurt)

✔ 1 part other natural waste (newspaper, tea bags, coffee grounds, eggshells, vegetable and fruit scraps)
micro-organisms + water + warmth + air + time

Place all ingredients in a large plastic bin in a sunny area as they become available. Next, sprinkle in some soil. Add more of each type of ingredient at any time they become available. Cover the bin with an old piece of carpet to allow air inside but to also keep the heat in. Add some water each week to moisten the mixture and stir the container with a shovel or large stick. When the compost is brown and crumbly it is ready to mix into your garden's soil. Mixing compost in your garden's soil feeds the soil and makes it strong and healthy.

CREATIVE
WRITING PROMPT
Write an article for the local newspaper to inform members of the community about the who, what, where, how and whys of recycling food waste by composting.

BOOKS
Casey's Compost
by Bonnie Bright

Compost Stew
by Mary McKenna Siddals

Garbage Helps Our Garden Grow: A Compost Story
by Linda Glaser

CREATIVE WRITING & PLANT NOTES

Plant:

Days Until Harvest:

Leaves:

Plant Height:

Growth Increase:

% Increase:

Are any leaves:

discolored   eaten   dry   broken

Is the plant:

dead   rotten   flowering   fruiting

Plant:

Days Until Harvest:

Leaves:

Plant Height:

Growth Increase:

% Increase:

Are any leaves:

discolored   eaten   dry   broken

Is the plant:

dead   rotten   flowering   fruiting

Lesson 11

ECOSYSTEM(noun):
an ecosystem can be looked at as a tiny world within our world

PROJECT:
MINI TERRARIUM ECOSYSTEMS

FOOD
FOR THE BRAIN

A mountain goat attempts to scale a cliff sixty feet high. Every minute, the goat bounds upward three feet but slips back two.

How long does it take for the goat to reach the top?

In an ecosystem, living things like plants, animals, and insects and non-living things including water, clouds, rocks, soil and temperature must all interact. Every part of the ecosystem influences and interacts with everything else in the ecosystem.

How living things and non-living things interact in an ecosystem:

Evaporate (verb):
turn from liquid into vapor (moisture in the air)

1. Water Cycling - A never ending continuous cycle where water evaporates, travels into the air and becomes part of a cloud, falls down to earth as precipitation (rain, snow, hail), and then evaporates again.

2. Primary Production - Plants that do not depend on other plants, animals, or insects for their food and only use help from the sun, water, and air is called primary production. Grass, dandelions and clovers are great examples of primary producers. Primary producers like plants make their own food by doing something called photosynthesis.

3. Consumption - Consumption is when something is eaten and a consumer is something that eats.

4. Decomposition - Decomposition is the process of allowing something (such as dead plants and the bodies of dead animals) to be slowly destroyed and broken down

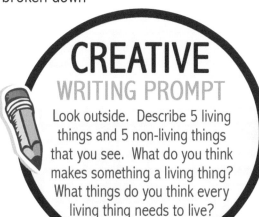

CREATIVE
WRITING PROMPT

Look outside. Describe 5 living things and 5 non-living things that you see. What do you think makes something a living thing? What things do you think every living thing needs to live?

BOOKS
Ecosystems at Risk
by Stephen Aitken

Amazing Biome Projects You Can Build Yourself
by Donna Latham

Ecosystems
by William Rice

CREATIVE WRITING & PLANT NOTES

Plant:
Days Until Harvest:
Leaves:
Plant Height:
Growth Increase:
% Increase:
Are any leaves:
discolored   eaten   dry   broken
Is the plant:
dead   rotten   flowering   fruiting

Plant:
Days Until Harvest:
Leaves:
Plant Height:
Growth Increase:
% Increase:
Are any leaves:
discolored   eaten   dry   broken
Is the plant:
dead   rotten   flowering   fruiting

BIODIVERSITY (noun):
the existence of many different kinds
of living things in an environment
or ecosystem

PROJECT:
PAPER MÂCHÉ EARTH GLOBES

FOOD
FOR THE BRAIN

There are 794 words in the word biodiversity. Find four of these words using the hints below.

_ _ _ S T _ _ _ _
To damage beyond repair

_ _ O _ B _ _
Mushy ice usually made with fruit juice

D _ B _
Something that is owed

_ _ R _ B _
A group of people sharing a common ancestry, culture and language

A healthy ecosystem has many types of living things including plants, animals, insects, fungi, and bacteria. Soil and water nurtures plants, animals eat plants, and animals are raised and used by humans for a variety of purposes. If one link of this chain were to go missing, the chain would be different or destroyed for all living things including humans.

Approximately 8.7 million different living species are found on earth, but due to human interactions, many species are disappearing. Humans need to protect and increase biodiversity in their ecosystems for reasons including:

1. Food - plants, animals and insects found around the world, including humans, feed on other plants, animals and insects

2. Air - plants use the air we breathe out (carbon dioxide) to feed themselves and in turn, provide the required oxygen for humans to breathe in

3. Medicine - most medicines come from plants and living micro-organisms such as bacteria and fungi

4. Building Materials - rubber, oil, fibers, dyes and adhesives (for example, glue) all come from natural resources

CREATIVE
WRITING PROMPT
Why is it important to protect biodiversity?

BOOKS
What If There Were No Sea Otters?: A Book About the Ocean Ecosystem
by Suzanne Slade

Tree of Life: The Incredible Biodiversity of Life on Earth
by Rochelle Strauss

CREATIVE WRITING & PLANT NOTES

Plant:	Plant:
Days Until Harvest:	Days Until Harvest:
# Leaves:	# Leaves:
Plant Height:	Plant Height:
Growth Increase:	Growth Increase:
% Increase:	% Increase:
Are any leaves:	Are any leaves:
discolored eaten dry broken	discolored eaten dry broken
Is the plant:	Is the plant:
dead rotten flowering fruiting	dead rotten flowering fruiting

EXTINCTION (adjective):
to no longer exist

PROJECT:
TOILET PAPER ROLL BIRD FEEDERS

FOOD
FOR THE BRAIN

Bluebirds are sitting in nine nests arranged in a three by three square. Connect each of the nine nests using only four straight lines and without lifting your pen from the paper.

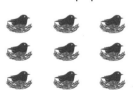

Any living thing can become <u>extinct</u>, which means that any and all ecosystems that it inhabits must change or risk dying out. Some of the major threats to biodiversity include:

• Over-Hunting - killing animals unnecessarily reduces their numbers and endangers their species

• Habitat Loss - when habitats, or homes for living things are demolished, the living things in that area are affected. For example, cutting down trees may be necessary to make way for new buildings and roads, but destroy habitats for living things at the same time

Native (adjective): born in a particular place

• Invasive Species - an invasive species can be any kind of living thing that is not native to an ecosystem and which causes harm. When a new species is introduced to a local ecosystem, the existing living things in the ecosystem must learn to adapt quickly or the entire ecosystem will be in chaos and living things that live there will face possible extinction. Why? One reason is that the new species may hog the food in the ecosystem, leaving little to no food for the existing native living things.

• Pollution - whether in the air, on land or in water, pollution is the process of making parts of the environment dirty and unsafe or unsuitable to use. From trash in the streets and in the ocean, to fumes in the air, pollution is harmful and threatens all living things.

CREATIVE
WRITING PROMPT

Pretend you are a vegetable seed waiting to be planted. Describe the type of seed you are, what vegetable you will produce, and give the gardener some tips to successfully grow you into a plant.

BOOKS

How a Seed Grows
by Helene J. Jordan

How Does a Seed Sprout?
by Melissa Stewart

Starting Seeds
by Barbara Ellis

Plant:	Plant:
Days Until Harvest:	Days Until Harvest:
# Leaves:	# Leaves:
Plant Height:	Plant Height:
Growth Increase:	Growth Increase:
% Increase:	% Increase:
Are any leaves:	Are any leaves:
discolored eaten dry broken	discolored eaten dry broken
Is the plant:	Is the plant:
dead rotten flowering fruiting	dead rotten flowering fruiting

PHOTOSYNTHESIS (verb):
simply put, photosynthesis is
sunlight + air people breathe out + water
= plant food + air people breathe in

PROJECT:
MIXED MEDIA
SUN ART

FOOD
FOR THE BRAIN

The teacher collected 5 green leaves in her basket. How can she divide the leaves among 5 children so that each child has 1 leaf while 1 leaf remains in the basket?

Plants that do not depend on other plants, animals, or insects for their food and only use help from the sun, water, and air is called primary production. Grass, dandelions and clovers are great examples of primary producers. Primary producers like plants make their own food by doing something called <u>photosynthesis</u>.

How does photosynthesis work?

- Leaves of plants absorb:
  - o Light from the sun
  - o Air that people breathe out, called carbon dioxide
  - o Water from falling rain or from the soil with their roots

- Leaves of plants use light from the sun to turn both the water and the air people breathe out (carbon dioxide!) into glucose and oxygen

- Glucose is a type of sugar that plants use for food help them grow

- Oxygen is the gas that people and animals breathe in. So not only do plants make their own food, but they make the air that we breathe in!

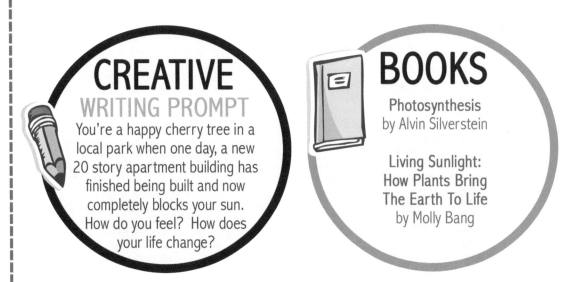

CREATIVE
WRITING PROMPT
You're a happy cherry tree in a local park when one day, a new 20 story apartment building has finished being built and now completely blocks your sun. How do you feel? How does your life change?

BOOKS
Photosynthesis
by Alvin Silverstein

Living Sunlight:
How Plants Bring
The Earth To Life
by Molly Bang

CREATIVE WRITING & PLANT NOTES

Plant:

Days Until Harvest:

Leaves:

Plant Height:

Growth Increase:

% Increase:

Are any leaves:

discolored   eaten   dry broken

Is the plant:

dead   rotten   flowering   fruiting

Plant:

Days Until Harvest:

Leaves:

Plant Height:

Growth Increase:

% Increase:

Are any leaves:

discolored   eaten   dry broken

Is the plant:

dead   rotten   flowering   fruiting

Lesson 15

CONSUMER(noun):
something or someone that eats or consumes things (use up)

PROJECT:
FOOD CHAIN BOOKMARKS

FOOD
FOR THE BRAIN

A farmer is taking a fox, a chicken, and a bag of grain home. To get there, he must cross a river, but he's only allowed to take one item across the bridge with him at a time. If the fox is left alone with the chicken, the fox will eat the chicken. If the chicken is left alone with the grain, the chicken will eat the grain. How can the farmer cross the river without any of his possessions being eaten?

Consumption is when something is eaten and a <u>consumer</u> is something that eats.

Animals and insects that eat other animals and insects are called carnivores, those that eat plants are called herbivores, and those that eat both animals, insects and plants are called omnivores.

Consumption is how all living things get their food so they can live and grow.

CREATIVE
WRITING PROMPT
Make up a funny fairy tale that involves something or someone being consumed.

BOOKS
Who Eats What?
by Patricia Lauber

Everybody's Somebodys Lunch
by Cherie Mason

Pass the Energy, Please!
by Barbara McKinney

Circle all the consumers in the picture below.

CREATIVE WRITING & PLANT NOTES

Plant:

Days Until Harvest:

Leaves:

Plant Height:

Growth Increase:

% Increase:

Are any leaves:

discolored eaten dry broken

Is the plant:

dead rotten flowering fruiting

Plant:

Days Until Harvest:

Leaves:

Plant Height:

Growth Increase:

% Increase:

Are any leaves:

discolored eaten dry broken

Is the plant:

dead rotten flowering fruiting

DECOMPOSE (verb):

scientific word for rot;
de- (reverse) + *compose* (put together)
means "to take something apart"

PROJECT:
COLORFUL PAINTED ROCK MANDALAS

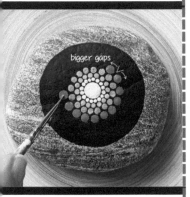

bigger gaps

FOOD
FOR THE BRAIN

Unscramble these words that also start with the "de" prefix:

ecttadieva

_____

tdnicaeeafefd

_____

atldeef

_____

herdotne

_____

Decomposition Process:

1. All living things eventually die including plants, animals, and insects.

2. Bacteria, fungi, and worms are called decomposers and need to eat some of the dead plants, animals, and insects so they can live and grow.

3. The tiny pieces left over after decomposers eat transform into nutrients for plants and become part of the soil.

4. Living plants take these nutrients from the soil so they can grow.

This process is called decomposition.

Common decomposers in your typical garden include bacteria, fungus, and earthworms.

CREATIVE
WRITING PROMPT

Earthworms are throwing a decomposition party! Write a story about the party and be sure to include details about the party food, music, favors and decorations.

BOOKS

Rotten Pumpkin
by David M. Schwartz

Rotters!: Decomposition
by John Townsend

Micro Life in Soil
by Natalie Hyde

CREATIVE WRITING & PLANT NOTES

Plant:

Days Until Harvest:

Leaves:

Plant Height:

Growth Increase:

% Increase:

Are any leaves:

discolored   eaten   dry broken

Is the plant:

dead rotten flowering fruiting

Plant:

Days Until Harvest:

Leaves:

Plant Height:

Growth Increase:

% Increase:

Are any leaves:

discolored   eaten   dry broken

Is the plant:

dead rotten flowering fruiting

Lesson 17

DORMANT (adjective):
asleep; temporarily inactive

PROJECT:
SEED COLLECTION ENVELOPE BOOKS

FOOD
FOR THE BRAIN

You just went to the garden nursery to buy some seeds with a bunch of change in your pocket. When you were ready to pay for your seeds, the cashier asked you a crazy question:

"What's the largest amount of money you can have in change and still not have change for a dollar?"

Seed Facts

• Seeds come in all shapes, sizes, colors, and textures

• Seeds contain all the material a plant needs for making more of itself

• When monocot seeds germinate, they start life with one seed leaf, like grass

• When dicot seeds germinate, they start life with two seed leaves, like beans

• Seeds have a protective coat that can be thin or thick, soft or hard

• The baby plant inside the seed is called the embryo

• Seeds can be spread by wind, water, and animals

• Most seeds remain <u>dormant</u> until they are given water

• Insects or other animals that transfer pollen from plant to plant are called pollinators

• Pollen is the fine, powder-like material plants need to make more seeds

CREATIVE
WRITING PROMPT
One day Jack went to play in his backyard when he found a tiny new tomato plant growing by his tree swing. Write a story about how that happened.

BOOKS
A Seed Is Sleepy
by Dianna Aston

Ride the Wind: Airborne Journeys of Animals and Plants
by Seymour Simon

How and Why Seeds Travel
by Elaine Pascoe

CREATIVE WRITING & PLANT NOTES

Plant:

Days Until Harvest:

Leaves:

Plant Height:

Growth Increase:

% Increase:

Are any leaves:

discolored   eaten   dry   broken

Is the plant:

dead   rotten   flowering   fruiting

Plant:

Days Until Harvest:

Leaves:

Plant Height:

Growth Increase:

% Increase:

Are any leaves:

discolored   eaten   dry   broken

Is the plant:

dead   rotten   flowering   fruiting

Lesson 18

LIFE CYCLE (noun):
the stages a living thing goes through during its life

PROJECT:
DRIED FLOWER BOOKMARKS

FOOD
FOR THE BRAIN

All the students in the class decided to make one large art piece with their bookmarks. Each bookmark measures 2.5" wide by 3" tall. If they had placed 6 rows of bookmarks with 4 bookmarks in each row (none were turned sideways), what would be the perimeter of the finished art piece? Hint: perimeter is width multiplied by height.

A plant's life cycle includes five main stages:

Seed Germination - Germination occurs when water is added to and absorbed by a seed, causing it to expand and split the seed open.

Sprout - Roots grow downward and anchor the plant to the soil while also enabling the plant to take the water and nutrients from the soil that is required for healthy plant growth. As the plant grows upward reaching for light, it becomes a sprout when it comes out of the soil and arrives at the surface.

Seedling - When the sprout grows its first green leaves, the plant becomes a seedling. Once the seedling develops these first leaves, it is able to make its own food and energy by using light through a process called photosynthesis.

Young Adult Plant - As the seedling grows and becomes stronger the seedling changes into a young adult plant with many leaves. Eventually the young plant will begin to produce buds that will in turn open up into flowers. Insects and birds then pollinate the flowers, allowing new seeds to be created in a process called fertilization.

Fruiting Plant - After pollination occurs, the flowers transform into fruiting bodies, which protect the numerous seeds that are inside. The flower petals eventually drop as seeds ripen. Once the seeds have dried, they are ready to be grown into new plants, repeating the life cycle of a flowering plant all over again. Often times, seeds are spread by animals eating the fruit and pooping out the seeds or by wind blowing them.

CREATIVE
WRITING PROMPT
You are a watermelon seed. Tell about your life growing up from a seed to a plant with watermelons.

BOOKS

Time For Kids: Plants!
by Editors of
TIME For Kids

National Geographic Readers:
Seed to Plant
by Kristin Baird Rattini

CREATIVE WRITING & PLANT NOTES

Plant:

Days Until Harvest:

Leaves:

Plant Height:

Growth Increase:

% Increase:

Are any leaves:

discolored eaten dry broken

Is the plant:

 dead rotten flowering fruiting

Plant:

Days Until Harvest:

Leaves:

Plant Height:

Growth Increase:

% Increase:

Are any leaves:

discolored eaten dry broken

Is the plant:

dead rotten flowering fruiting

Lesson 19

FUNCTION (verb):
an action performed by somebody or something that produces a result

PROJECT:
TREE OF LIFE WITH NOTES & QUOTES

FOOD
FOR THE BRAIN

Unscramble 4 words found on this page related to plants parts and their functions:

tieitfnlioraz

_____

yhtonshsptoies

_____

treamgein

_____

velase

_____

The basic parts of almost all plants include roots, stems, leaves, flowers, fruits, and seeds and each of these parts has their own special <u>function</u>:

Roots - Roots grow downward and anchor the plant to the soil while also enabling the plant to take the water and nutrients from the soil that is required for growth.

Stems - Stems carry water and nutrients taken up by the roots to the leaves. They also are a strong part of the plant that can provide the necessary support for the plant so the leaves can reach the sunlight that they need to produce food.

Leaves - Through photosynthesis, leaves catch light and have openings to allow water and air to come and go, making all the food and energy needed for plants to grow.

Flowers - Flowers are where seeds are made. Beautifully colored and fragrant flower petals attract pollinators such as bees, birds and butterflies to the flower where they drink or collect nectar. At the same time, they get covered in sticky pollen and the flowers are pollinated when some of the pollen from the first flower sticks to the second flower, creating fruit and seeds in a process called fertilization.

Fruits - The fruit is either fleshy or hard and dry to protect the developing seeds. Every seed is a tiny plant with leaves, stems, and root parts waiting for water and the right situation to germinate and grow.

Seeds - Seeds are protected by a coat that helps it survive until it has water and the right conditions to germinate and become a plant. Often times, seeds are spread by animals eating the fruit and pooping out the seeds, by wind blowing them, or from water moving them.

CREATIVE
WRITING PROMPT
You are water. Describe your journey through a plant.

BOOKS

Plant Parts
by Louise Spilsbury and Richard Spilsbury

Plant Parts Smarts: Science Adventures with Charlie the Origami Bee
by Eric Braun

CREATIVE WRITING & PLANT NOTES

Plant:
Days Until Harvest:
Leaves:
Plant Height:
Growth Increase:
% Increase:
Are any leaves:
discolored eaten dry broken
Is the plant:
dead rotten flowering fruiting

Plant:
Days Until Harvest:
Leaves:
Plant Height:
Growth Increase:
% Increase:
Are any leaves:
discolored eaten dry broken
Is the plant:
dead rotten flowering fruiting

POLLEN (noun):
fine, powdery, yellowish grains in flowers that causes plants to form seeds, and new plants to grow from the seeds

PROJECT:
PAPER FLOWERS

FOOD
FOR THE BRAIN

I have more than two flowers in my bouquet. All of them are roses, except for two. All of them are tulips, except for two. All of them are daisies, except for two.

What kinds of flowers are in my bouquet and how many of each type of flower do I have?

Pollination is how pollinators help plants to make seeds through the act of transferring pollen from one plant to another. Pollinators play a very important role in the life cycle of plants. Pollination is crucial to life on our planet.

Birds, bees, butterflies, bats and ladybugs are a few of the world's most helpful pollinators. On flowering plants, the bright colors and smells of flowers attract pollinators and entice them to drink their sugary nectar. While eating, some pollen rubs off on the pollinator by accident. When the pollinator moves to sip nectar from another plant's flower, the pollen from the first flower will rub off, fertilizing the flower's egg cells to make seeds.

Wind is also an important pollinator, taking pollen between flowering plants, and helping the plants make seeds.

When a plant makes new seeds, the plant can then reproduce and create new plants (ah, babies!). This is important because plants provide humans and animals with the food, shelter and the oxygen all living things breathe and need to survive.

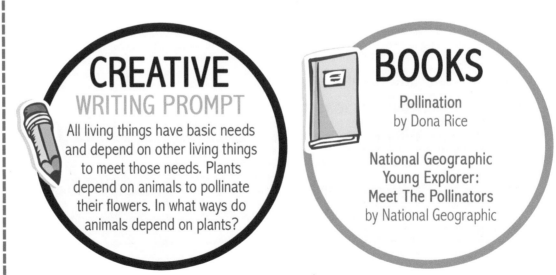

CREATIVE
WRITING PROMPT
All living things have basic needs and depend on other living things to meet those needs. Plants depend on animals to pollinate their flowers. In what ways do animals depend on plants?

BOOKS
Pollination
by Dona Rice

National Geographic
Young Explorer:
Meet The Pollinators
by National Geographic

CREATIVE WRITING & PLANT NOTES

Plant:	Plant:
Days Until Harvest:	Days Until Harvest:
# Leaves:	# Leaves:
Plant Height:	Plant Height:
Growth Increase:	Growth Increase:
% Increase:	% Increase:
Are any leaves:	Are any leaves:
discolored eaten dry broken	discolored eaten dry broken
Is the plant:	Is the plant:
dead rotten flowering fruiting	dead rotten flowering fruiting

POLLINATOR(noun):
a living or non-living thing that moves pollen from one plant to another to produce more plants or fruits

PROJECT:
FELT CIRCLE & RIBBON BIRDS

FOOD
FOR THE BRAIN

One day a mama and papa bird found a fresh compost pile full of juicy, delicious worms and decided to invite their entire family to take part in the worm feast: one grandfather, one grandmother, two fathers, two mothers, four children, three grandchildren, one brother, two sisters, two sons, two daughters, one father-in-law, one mother-in-law, and one daughter-in-law. But not as many people attended as it sounds. How many were there, and who were they?

Birds are found nearly everywhere. Birds are animals that have feathers on them and lay eggs. There are nearly 10,000 types of birds on our planet.

Creating a bird friendly garden with flowers, seeds, water and natural materials is important to maintaining biodiversity.

Birds need plants for food, nesting sites, and protection from predators.

Birds eat lots of things including worms, insects, fish, nectar, berries, and seeds and are a natural way to control pests in our gardens.

When a bird eats berries and then poops, the berry seeds are disposed of and given an opportunity to germinate and make new plants. The bird poop also makes a great natural fertilizer that provides nutrients for plants.

Some birds are important pollinators. A bird can do the same pollination job done by bees by simply landing on a plant or sucking the nectar from a flower and then moving on to the next flower.

All birds have different kinds of habitats. Some live in trees, some live in forests, some live in houses, and some live in the grass. Other birds live in water like ducks, swans, and geese, while some live on the ground like an ostrich and emu.

CREATIVE
WRITING PROMPT
You are a bird. Describe what kind of bird you are and tell us about your daily life.

BOOKS
Extreme Birds: The World's Most Extraordinary & Bizarre by Dominic Couzens

National Geographic Field Guide to the Birds of North America by J. Dunn & J. Alderfer

----

Plant:	Plant:
Days Until Harvest:	Days Until Harvest:
# Leaves:	# Leaves:
Plant Height:	Plant Height:
Growth Increase:	Growth Increase:
% Increase:	% Increase:
Are any leaves:	**Are any leaves:**
discolored eaten dry broken	discolored eaten dry broken
Is the plant:	**Is the plant:**
dead rotten flowering fruiting	dead rotten flowering fruiting

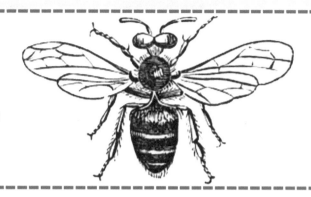

INSECTS (noun):
a small arthropod animal that has six legs and generally one or two pairs of wings

PROJECT:
UPCYCLED WINE CORK PENDANTS

QUICK
QUESTIONS

A beekeeper has an 8-gallon container full of honey he harvested from his backyard beehives. He also has two empty containers that measure 5 gallons and 3 gallons. He needs to deliver 4 gallons of honey to a customer. The beekeeper has no other spare containers and no way to mark any containers. He does not want to pour honey away. How will he measure the 4 gallons of honey?

Bees are <u>insects</u> that fly around all day with the goal of bringing nectar back to their hives to turn it into honey. So as bees travel from blossom to blossom to drink and collect nectar from the flowers, they get covered in sticky pollen. Some of the pollen from the first flower sticks to the second flower and so on. In this way, the flowers are pollinated.

Most plants that flower contain nectar and attract bees. Red flowers do not attract bees because bees do not see the color red and the red flowers appear black to them.

Bees are responsible for pollinating the plants that produce many of the fruits and vegetables we eat. Almost all of the produce you eat depends on honeybee pollination and the produce section of a grocery store would be quite empty without bees. Apple, cherry and cranberry growers would lose 60-80% of their crops without honeybees.

Our world's honeybee population continues to decline. The reasons are not exactly clear, but John Schwartz of The New York Times said, "What has emerged is a complex set of pressures on managed and wild bee populations that includes disease, a parasite known as the varroa mite, pesticides, extreme weather and poor nutrition tied to a loss of forage plants."

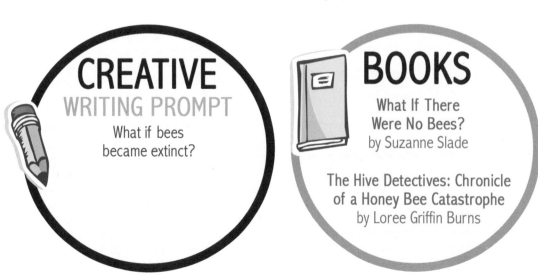

CREATIVE
WRITING PROMPT
What if bees became extinct?

BOOKS
What If There Were No Bees?
by Suzanne Slade

The Hive Detectives: Chronicle of a Honey Bee Catastrophe
by Loree Griffin Burns

CREATIVE WRITING & PLANT NOTES

Plant:

Days Until Harvest:

Leaves:

Plant Height:

Growth Increase:

% Increase:

Are any leaves:

discolored eaten dry broken

Is the plant:

dead rotten flowering fruiting

Plant:

Days Until Harvest:

Leaves:

Plant Height:

Growth Increase:

% Increase:

Are any leaves:

discolored eaten dry broken

Is the plant:

dead rotten flowering fruiting

Lesson 23

URBANIZATION (noun):
the process by which towns and cities are formed and become larger as more and more people begin living and working

PROJECT:
ARTIST TRADING CARDS

FOOD
FOR THE BRAIN

Janie did some research on the lifespan of butterflies. She discovered that Painted Ladies live approximately 12 months, Monarchs for about 33 weeks, and a small Costa Rican butterfly for only 4 days. How long do butterflies live on average based only on the 3 types of butterflies from Janie's research? Hint: Average is defined as the sum of all the given elements divided by the total number of elements.

Butterflies are insects that are found nearly everywhere. There are nearly 28,000 types of butterflies on our planet.

Most butterflies live for only a few weeks while some can live for up to a year.

Almost all butterflies sip nectar from flowers through their tongues, which act like little straws. Different types of butterflies have different preferences of nectar in both color and taste. To attract and entice the greatest diversity of butterfly visitors to your garden, you will need to plant a wide variety of plants with flowers that produce lots of nectar.

Butterflies are pollinators like birds and bees, spreading pollen from flower to flower, leading to fertilization and ultimately seed production so new plants can grow.

The numbers of butterflies are being reduced in alarming rates because of pollution and <u>urbanization</u> destroying their homes.

CREATIVE
WRITING PROMPT
If you were a butterfly, describe in vivid detail what colors you would be and places you would like to fly to.

BOOKS
Butterflies: Pollinators and Nectar Sippers
by Adele D. Richardson

Smithsonian Handbooks: Butterflies & Moths
by David J. Carter

Plant:

Days Until Harvest:

Leaves:

Plant Height:

Growth Increase:

% Increase:

Are any leaves:

discolored   eaten   dry   broken

Is the plant:

dead   rotten   flowering   fruiting

Plant:

Days Until Harvest:

Leaves:

Plant Height:

Growth Increase:

% Increase:

Are any leaves:

discolored   eaten   dry   broken

Is the plant:

dead   rotten   flowering   fruiting

NOCTURNAL (adjective):
most likely to come out
at night or very early
in the morning

PROJECT:
POLYMER CLAY SNAIL DECORATIONS

FOOD
FOR THE BRAIN

A snail creeps 9 feet up a wall at night. When the daylight comes, the snail sleeps. The next evening it wakes up and discovers that it slipped down 6 feet while sleeping. If this happens every day, how many days will the snail take to reach the top of a wall 60 feet in height? And why do you think the snail is on the move at night instead of during the day?

Snails are small animals that are mostly <u>nocturnal</u>, with some living for 15 to 25 years depending on the type of snail.

The common garden snail is considered a garden pest as it eats the leaves and stems of crops. The majority of snails are herbivores eating leaves, stems and flowers, while some species are omnivores or carnivores, eating other animals or insects.

Common garden snails have a top speed of 50-60 yards (half a football field) per hour, making the snail one of the slowest creatures on the planet.

As a snail moves, they leave behind a trail of mucus, which acts as a lubricant to slide along and keep moving. This also allows the snail to move along upside down.

There is no way to tell whether a snail is a male or a female because they are both - in biology, the word hermaphrodite is used to describe this characteristic.

The snail is a delicacy in French cuisine called escargot (pronounced *es-car-goat*).

The expression "snail's pace" is a term used to describe something or somebody that is extremely slow and "snail mail" is now commonly used when referring to sending regular mail rather than that sent by email.

CREATIVE
WRITING PROMPT
You are a snail.
Tell the story of your life:
where you were born,
your name,
where you have been,
what you eat…

BOOKS
The Snail Who Forgot The Mail
by Sigal Adler

Snails, Shellfish, and Other Mollusks
by Daniel Gilpin

Snails
by Kevin Holmes

CREATIVE WRITING & PLANT NOTES

Plant:

Days Until Harvest:

Leaves:

Plant Height:

Growth Increase:

% Increase:

Are any leaves:

discolored eaten dry broken

Is the plant:

dead rotten flowering fruiting

Plant:

Days Until Harvest:

Leaves:

Plant Height:

Growth Increase:

% Increase:

Are any leaves:

discolored eaten dry broken

Is the plant:

dead rotten flowering fruiting

DECOMPOSER (noun):
any living thing that eats dead plants, animals, and insects so they can live and grow

PROJECT:
WOOL BOOKWORM BOOKMARKS

Garden worms are called earthworms and are a valuable addition to a healthy garden.

Earthworms are <u>decomposers</u> that eat dead plants, animals, and insects so they can live and grow. And when the worms poops the remains of these dead plants, animals, and insects, it makes the soil rich with valuable nutrients including nitrogen, phosphorous, potassium, and magnesium that plants love and need for growth and fruit production.

Earthworms also loosen the soil which makes it easier for plant roots to grow and for the air and water to circulate in the soil. This helps the soil retain the proper amount of air and water for healthy plants to grow.

Smart gardeners provide a good environment for earthworms to grow and multiply. This means keeping your garden soil moist and adding lots of organic matter through things like compost because that's what worms love to eat.

FOOD
FOR THE BRAIN

There can only be 15 worms in any given row, column, or diagonal of a three by three square. Arrange the numbers 1 through 9 on a three by three square such that the numbers in each row, column, and diagonal add up to 15.

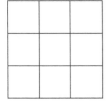

CREATIVE
WRITING PROMPT
Write a poem about worms using at least 10 words that start with the letter W. Use the dictionary for W word inspiration! Wowzers!

BOOKS
Wiggling Worms at Work
by Wendy Pfeffer

Life in a Bucket of Soil
by Alvin Silverstein

Plant:

Days Until Harvest:

Leaves:

Plant Height:

Growth Increase:

% Increase:

Are any leaves:

discolored eaten dry broken

Is the plant:

dead rotten flowering fruiting

Plant:

Days Until Harvest:

Leaves:

Plant Height:

Growth Increase:

% Increase:

Are any leaves:

discolored eaten dry broken

Is the plant:

dead rotten flowering fruiting

PREVENTION(noun): an action to prevent something from happening

PROJECT:
CIRCLE OF LIFE PLANT FLIPBOOK

FOOD
FOR THE BRAIN

Unscramble the names of these common garden pests:

slina
lebeet
idhpa
aieplcrlatr
omht

One day you might go out to your garden only to find holes chewed in leaves or plants wilting and yellowing. What happened? Well, a pest or disease may be to blame! Now what do you do? If you see pests or signs of harmful insects and disease, address the problem ASAP:

• Wear gloves and pick the pests off the plants and soil and move them to another location away from your garden

• Pick off and trash infected leaves (don't put them in compost bins)

• Insects, mites, slugs, and snails are major pests of vegetable and fruit crops

• Remember that although pests are "pesty" and may cause you and your garden problems, there are really no "bad bugs" - in a healthy ecosystem, all creatures have value and have an important role to play

The best offense to garden pests and diseases is a good defense. Here are some ways to <u>prevent</u> pests in your garden before they happen:

1. Eat Right! - Just like humans who eat a nutritious diet and get quality exercise and rest are less likely to get sick, plants are better able to fend off pests and diseases when they have healthy soil with compost added regularly.

2. Soil Moisture - Always try to make sure your soil is consistently and evenly moist. Not too wet and not too dry. Try to avoid getting the tops of plants wet when you water as wet leaves and stems promote the development of many diseases.

3. I Need My Space! - Crowded plants trap water and encourage diseases so space plants out when you plant them so there is good air circulation around them.

4. Flowers Welcome! - Plant some flowers along with your fruits and vegetables to attract birds and other beneficial insects that can help eat unwanted pests.

5. Maintain Your Garden - Remove weeds when you see them crop up. Weeds not only compete with your crops for nutrients, light, and water, but some weeds also make cozy homes for pests that attack garden crops as well.

BOOKS
The Vegetable Gardener's Container Bible
by Edward C. Smith

All New Square Foot Gardening, 2nd Edition: The Revolutionary Way to Grow More In Less Space
by Mel Bartholomew

CREATIVE
WRITING PROMPT
Your doorbell rings. You answer the door and find a slug wearing a suit and tie. He confesses that he's been eating the broccoli plants in your garden. Tell the rest of the story.

Plant:

Days Until Harvest:

Leaves:

Plant Height:

Growth Increase:

% Increase:

Are any leaves:

discolored   eaten   dry broken

Is the plant:

dead rotten flowering fruiting

Plant:

Days Until Harvest:

Leaves:

Plant Height:

Growth Increase:

% Increase:

Are any leaves:

discolored   eaten   dry broken

Is the plant:

dead rotten flowering fruiting

FUNGI (noun):
organisms that live by decomposing and digesting the organic material in which they grow

PROJECT:
MINI CLAY MUSHROOMS

FOOD
FOR THE BRAIN

There are four, three letter words in the word *fungi* that start with the letter F. What are they?

_____

_____

_____

_____

Unlike green plants, which produce food energy through photosynthesis in the presence of sunlight, <u>fungi</u> are decomposers that derive their energy by digesting dead plants, insects and animals.

As fungi eats dead plants, insects and animals, they release valuable nutrients back into the soil that can be used again by plants.

Fungi is one of the top garbage eaters on the planet, recycling millions of tons of organic waste annually.

A <u>spore</u> is created by fungi and is like a seed that can produce new fungi.

Mushrooms, molds, mildews, rusts, and yeasts are common types of fungi.

Never attempt to eat any mushroom that you find anywhere unless it came from the grocery store. Many mushrooms look like the ones you see in the grocery store but are deadly when consumed! So even if you are 99% sure you can make the correct identification of a mushroom, mushroom poisoning is one of the most horrible deaths known to man and is not worth the risk if you're wrong.

CREATIVE
WRITING PROMPT
Fungus amongus!
Write a rhyming poem about fungus using the following words: fungus, humongous, spaghetti, Betty, confetti, ready, braids, grades, shades, parades

BOOKS

The Fungus That Ate My School
by Arthur Dorros

Molds, Mushrooms & Other Fungi
by Steve Parker

CREATIVE WRITING & PLANT NOTES

Plant:
Days Until Harvest:
Leaves:
Plant Height:
Growth Increase:
% Increase:
Are any leaves:
discolored eaten dry broken
Is the plant:
dead rotten flowering fruiting

Plant:
Days Until Harvest:
Leaves:
Plant Height:
Growth Increase:
% Increase:
Are any leaves:
discolored eaten dry broken
Is the plant:
dead rotten flowering fruiting

Lesson 28

HARVEST (noun):
a time when ripened crops are picked and gathered

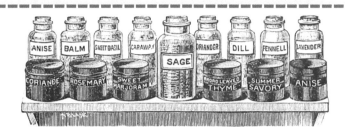

PROJECT:
STRAWBERRY POTPOURRI SACHETS

FOOD
FOR THE BRAIN

Martha wanted to make fresh blueberry pancakes for breakfast but she only had 9 minutes before she had to leave for school. If each pancake took 3 minutes to cook on each side, and her pan could only cook 2 pancakes at a time, what's the most amount of pancakes could she make before she had to leave for school?

You should know an estimated time to harvest the fruits and vegetables in your garden as well as what the ripe fruits and vegetables should look like based on the descriptions and information the back of the seed packets for your plants (hopefully you will have written this information in your garden planner from Lesson 1).

Whenever possible, pick your fruits and vegetables when they are bright in color, ripe, and ready to be eaten. This will ensure you have the most nutrients and flavor.

Be sure to wash fruits and vegetables thoroughly, especially green leafy vegetables. This way, you ensure them free from dirt and any cute little bugs that may have found a home in your plants. And toss any fruits and vegetables with weird spots, holes or mold.

If you have excess ripe fruits and vegetables, consider giving some away to friends and family, drying them for snacks, freezing, or canning them.

If you have extra herbs, cut and hang them to dry for later for use in cooking, for tea, and as potpourri for pretty smelling crafts.

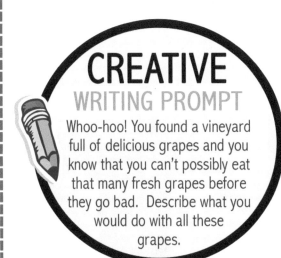

CREATIVE
WRITING PROMPT
Whoo-hoo! You found a vineyard full of delicious grapes and you know that you can't possibly eat that many fresh grapes before they go bad. Describe what you would do with all these grapes.

BOOKS
Garden Harvest
by Steven Bradley

Strega Nona's Harvest
by Tomie dePaola

Preserving Summer's Bounty
by Susan McClure

CREATIVE WRITING & PLANT NOTES

Plant:

Days Until Harvest:

Leaves:

Plant Height:

Growth Increase:

% Increase:

Are any leaves:

discolored eaten dry broken

Is the plant:

dead rotten flowering fruiting

Plant:

Days Until Harvest:

Leaves:

Plant Height:

Growth Increase:

% Increase:

Are any leaves:

discolored eaten dry broken

Is the plant:

dead rotten flowering fruiting

ANNUAL, BIENNIAL, OR PERENNIAL (adjectives):

all plants can be classified as either annual, biennial, or perennial - annuals live for only one growing season, during which they produce seeds, then die; biennials live for two growing seasons; perennials live for more than two years

PROJECT:
PINECONE GNOMES

FOOD
FOR THE BRAIN

Mila and Mischa were crafting up pinecone gnomes one afternoon when Mila said "I was just thinking, Mischa. If you gave me one of your gnomes, then we would have the same number of gnomes." Mischa replied, "Well, how about this instead....if you gave me one of your gnomes, then I would have twice as many as you!" How many gnomes does Mila have and how many gnomes does Mischa have?

Aquatic Plants - Aquatic plants live in water, providing a protective cover, oxygen and food for fish.

Berried Plants - Berried plants grow in most parts of the country and produce juicy, rounded, brightly colored, pulpy fruits called berries, many which are delicious and edible, and many that are extremely poisonous.

Bulb Plants - A bulb plant is any plant that stores its complete life cycle in an underground storage structure. They have a period of growth and flowering followed by a period of dormancy (sleep!) where they die back to ground level at the end of each growing season. Popular bulb plants include onions and tulips.

Climbing Plants - Climbing plants are very flexible and strong because they use other plants, rocks or manmade structures to climb on and provide support. Grapes and ivy are some of the most well known climbing plants.

Grasses - Grasses are one of the most important plants because of their strong root systems and for the nutritious grains they provide to humans and animals including corn, wheat, and rice. Sugarcane is a grass that supplies most of the world's sugar.

Succulent Plants - By definition, the word "succulent" means juicy. A succulent plant is able to store water to help it survive in hot temperatures and dry conditions. Popular succulents include cactus, agave, aloe vera and pineapple.

Trees - Trees provide important habitats for many animals as well as provide humans with many products, such as fruits, nuts, wood, and medicine. Trees are either deciduous (for example, oak trees), losing their leaves each year, or evergreen, with leaves or needles (for example, pine trees) that last for years.

CREATIVE
WRITING PROMPT

If you could be any kind of plant, what kind would you be and why? Where would you be planted? What would you look like? Would you have flowers? Would you bear fruit? Tell us!

BOOKS

Poisonous, Smelly, and Amazing Plants
by Zondervan

A-Z Encyclopedia of Garden Plants
by The American Horticultural Society

CREATIVE WRITING & PLANT NOTES

Plant:

Days Until Harvest:

Leaves:

Plant Height:

Growth Increase:

% Increase:

Are any leaves:

discolored eaten dry broken

Is the plant:

dead rotten flowering fruiting

Plant:

Days Until Harvest:

Leaves:

Plant Height:

Growth Increase:

% Increase:

Are any leaves:

discolored eaten dry broken

Is the plant:

dead rotten flowering fruiting

Lesson 30

NUTRITION (noun):
food; nourishment used by living things for growth and repair

PROJECT:
PAPER MÂCHÉ WATERMELON BOWL

FOOD
FOR THE BRAIN

An old cherry tree is four times as old as the younger, newer cherry tree. In twenty years, the old cherry tree will be twice as old as the new cherry tree.

How old are they both now?

Fruits and vegetables have been in the human diet for all of human history and as you I'm sure you already know, fruits and vegetables are just plain awesome!

Here are a few reasons why:
• Fruits and vegetables can be great sources of key nutrients that play a role in reducing the risk of certain diseases including heart disease, high blood pressure, and some cancers.

• Fruits and vegetables provide an amazing source of fiber that help fill you up and keep your digestive system happy. In plain language, this means that they help you poop as easy, often and as much as you should!

• Fruits and vegetables are <u>nutritious</u> and convenient to eat in any form - fresh, frozen, canned, dried, or juiced!

• Fruits and vegetables are naturally low in calories, making it an delicious no-brainer snack or great addition to any meal.

• Fruits and vegetables are rich in vitamins and minerals like potassium, calcium, iron, vitamin A and vitamin C that help you feel healthy and energized.

• Fruits and vegetables make you smile because they are colorful, delicious and nutritious!

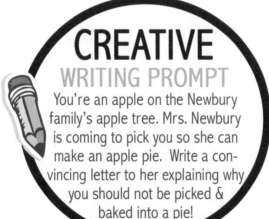

CREATIVE
WRITING PROMPT
You're an apple on the Newbury family's apple tree. Mrs. Newbury is coming to pick you so she can make an apple pie. Write a convincing letter to her explaining why you should not be picked & baked into a pie!

BOOKS
How a Seed Grows
by Helene J. Jordan

How Does a Seed Sprout?
by Melissa Stewart

Starting Seeds
by Barbara Ellis

Plant:

Days Until Harvest:

Leaves:

Plant Height:

Growth Increase:

% Increase:

Are any leaves:

discolored   eaten   dry   broken

Is the plant:

dead   rotten   flowering   fruiting

Plant:

Days Until Harvest:

Leaves:

Plant Height:

Growth Increase:

% Increase:

Are any leaves:

discolored   eaten   dry   broken

Is the plant:

dead   rotten   flowering   fruiting

Lesson 31

CULTURE (noun):
the sum of attitudes, customs, and beliefs that distinguishes one group of people from another

PROJECT:
WHO GROWS WHAT WHERE? MAPS

FOOD
FOR THE BRAIN

Three humans and three monkeys (one big, two small) need to cross a river. But there is only one boat, and it can only hold two bodies t(regardless of their size), and only the humans or the big monkey are strong enough to row the boat. Furthermore, the number of monkeys can never outnumber the number of humans on the same side of the river, or the monkeys will attack the humans. How can all six get across the river without anyone getting hurt?

Food is a basic human need that ties us to our environments.

The food we grow locally depends on our local climate and terrain. For example, is the weather mostly sunny, dry, or rainy? Is the soil sandy, muddy or full of clay? Are there thick forests or lots of grasslands nearby? The climate and terrain is the number one influence on the type of food grown and consumed in a region because that determines what plants can grow successfully there.

Local food creates a modern <u>culture</u> for people that live there, defining popular and familiar dishes prepared in local homes and restaurants. Plus local seasonal fruits and vegetables are fresher, are more flavorful, cost less, and don't contribute to pollution because they don't need to be transported long distances.

What one eats can also say a lot about who we are as individuals, and where we come from. For example, many meals we cook and eat may also use ingredients grown elsewhere in the world. Based on where those ingredients are grown, one may have insight to one's culture and personal family history.

CREATIVE
WRITING PROMPT
Humans decided to move to another planet and sell planet Earth. Write an ad for selling Earth. Describe some of the amazing food that exists on our planet as a selling point.

BOOKS
How Did That Get Here?
A series of 17+ nonfiction picture books titled
The Biography of...
and features a different food or agricultural product

Plant:

Days Until Harvest:

Leaves:

Plant Height:

Growth Increase:

% Increase:

Are any leaves:

discolored   eaten   dry   broken

Is the plant:

dead   rotten   flowering   fruiting

Plant:

Days Until Harvest:

Leaves:

Plant Height:

Growth Increase:

% Increase:

Are any leaves:

discolored   eaten   dry   broken

Is the plant:

dead   rotten   flowering   fruiting

GMO / GENETICALLY MODIFIED ORGANISM (noun):

a laboratory process where scientists take two similar plants or animals and combine them so they produce a new plant or animal with the most desirable characteristics

PROJECT:
MR. RECYCLE HEAD PLANTER

FOOD
FOR THE BRAIN

The Punnett square is a grid diagram genetic scientists use to predict what genes (eye color, height, etc) the child of two parents will have, whether it is a plant, human or another animal. Based on the information and Punnett square below, what is the probability that the child pea plant would come out small if a tall pea plant (Tt) was mixed with a short one (tt)?

	T	t
t	Tt	tt
t	Tt	tt

T = dominant tall plant gene

t = recessive small plant gene

TT = tall plant
Tt = tall plant
tt = short plant

Agricultural biotechnology scientists have found ways to take desirable qualities from one plant and put them into another plant to create seeds that will grow into new plants that are more nutritious and more resistant to pests so more food can be produced. Some seeds are also designed to allow plants to be grown year round in any climate while others are designed simply to help fruit to "look better." For example, new apple varieties have been developed that don't turn brown for an entire two weeks after slicing. And dairy cows are injected with the genetically engineered hormone rBGH that increase milk production. GMOs have generated plenty of debate, with some saying these foods are bad for our health and the environment, while others say the opposite.

Possible benefits:
• Plants may have shorter growing cycles and higher yields, which means more food can be produced in less time, helping to feed people in countries that may not have enough food to feed the people who live there

• Plants may have a stronger resistance to both pests and disease, which means less plants die from pests and diseases and more food can be produced

• Plants may be more nutritious

• Plants may have a longer shelf life at grocery stores, meaning less wasted food

Possible consequences:
• Plants are modified to "automatically" include toxic poisons designed to reduce the risk of pests and diseases killing the plants, but these toxic poisons may harmful to humans when consumed

• Plants may end up harming birds, bees, insects, amphibians, and soil organisms because they impact their health and ability to reproduce

• New "superbugs" and "superweeds" have evolved to beat these new plants designed to stop pests and diseases from eating them

Evolved (verb): develop gradually, especially from a simple to a more complex form

CREATIVE
WRITING PROMPT
You are a scientist who genetically modifies food and have been asked to create the ultimate food plant. What characteristics of existing animals and/or plants would you combine to create this new food?

BOOKS
Look Closer at Biotechnology Activity Book
by The Council for Biotechnology

Genetically Modified Foods vs. Sustainability
by Bruno McGrath

CREATIVE WRITING & PLANT NOTES

Plant:	Plant:
Days Until Harvest:	Days Until Harvest:
# Leaves:	# Leaves:
Plant Height:	Plant Height:
Growth Increase:	Growth Increase:
% Increase:	% Increase:
Are any leaves:	Are any leaves:
discolored eaten dry broken	discolored eaten dry broken
Is the plant:	Is the plant:
dead rotten flowering fruiting	dead rotten flowering fruiting

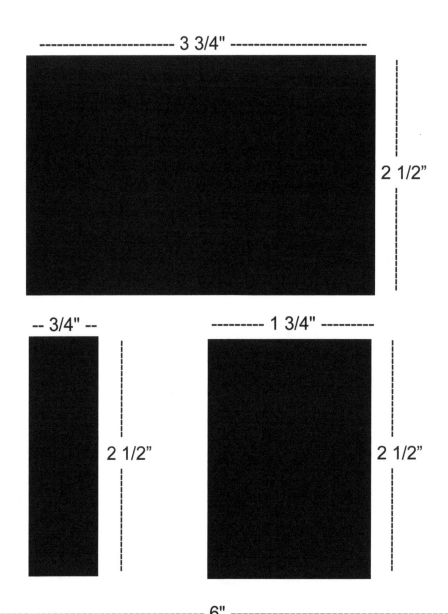

--------------------- 3 3/4" ---------------------

2 1/2"

-- 3/4" --

2 1/2"

--------- 1 3/4" ---------

2 1/2"

------------------------------ 6" ------------------------------

CUT 2 AND TAPE TOGETHER TO MAKE
A 12" x 2 1/2" TEMPLATE

2 1/2"

IMAGES

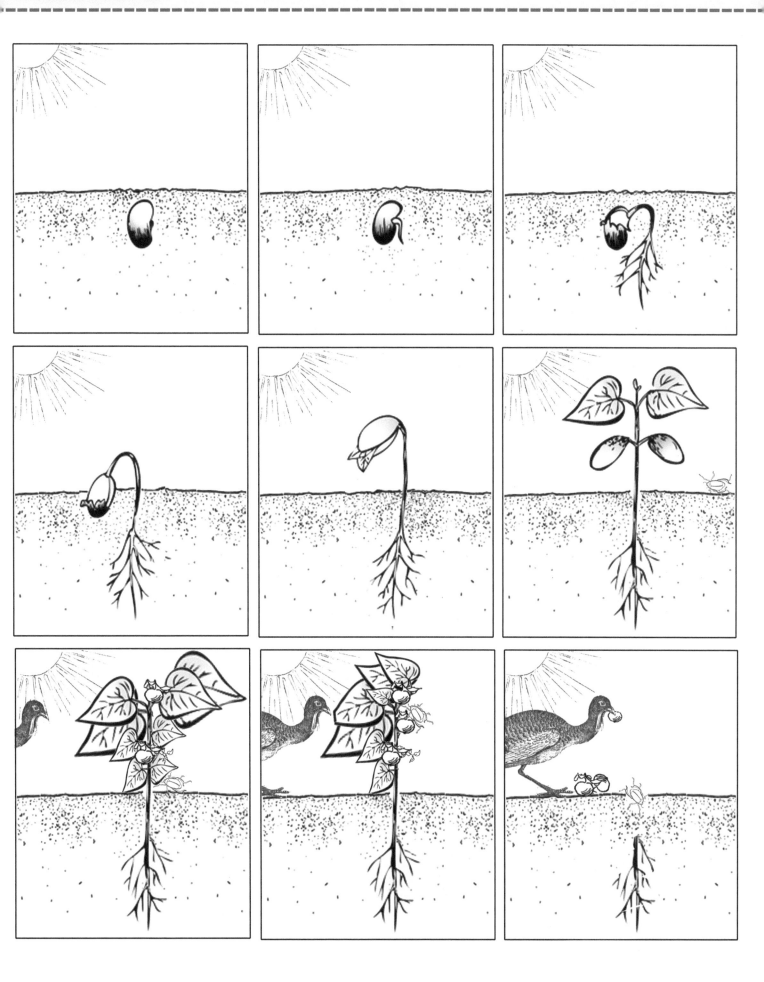

CUT-OUT

✂ ┄┄┄┄┄┄┄┄┄ cut here

IMAGES

bacteria   fungi   worms

FOOD FOR THE BRAIN

- 41 years ago, when Martha's tree was 13 and her mother's tree was 39

- Three - one rose, one tulip, and one daisy

- Who cares? I want to see how that half a girl can eat anything. But....let's break the question down into steps. We know that a girl and a half can eat a pineapple and a half in a minute and a half. So how many pineapples could six girls eat in a minute and a half? We have the same amount of time, but four times as many girls, so the answer is four times as many pineapples. Six, to be precise. But now let's consider what six girls could eat in six minutes. We now have four times as much time, so the answer is four times as many pineapples -- specifically, 24.

- To get seven gallons, fill the five gallon jug and dump what you can into the three gallon jug, filling it. There are now two gallons in the five gallon jug. Dump out the three gallon jug, and put the two gallons from the five gallon jug into the three gallon jug. Then fill the five gallon jug. The total is seven gallons.

- There's the same amount of lemonade in the orange juice as orange juice in the lemonade. Each cup ends with the same volume of liquid that it started with, and there's still an equal amount of each juice between the two cups.

- Three. In the worst case, the first two gloves you take out will consist of one blue glove and one gray glove. The next glove you take out is guaranteed to match one or the other.

- Short

- Seven

- None

- Fifty eight minutes. Although his net progress each minute is one foot, he reaches the top on the fifty-eighth minute just before he would normally slip back two feet.

- destroy, sorbet, debts, tribe

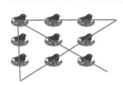

- 4 children get 1 leaf each while the 5th child gets the basket with the remaining leaf still in it.

- Take the chicken across and leave it on the other side. Then go back. Get the fox and bring it to the other side and take the chicken back with you. Take the grain to the other side and leave it there. Then go back and get the chicken.

- deactivate, decaffeinated, deflate, dethrone

- **$1.19. Three quarters, four dimes, and four pennies.** Think about the question - we are looking for the greatest amount of money you can have in coins but not be able to make exactly one dollar from any combination of those coins. Start with largest value coin, the quarter, and take as many as possible without being able to make exactly $1 worth of change. Next, move on to the dime, then the nickel, then the penny. Quarters: 4 quarter is $1, so you can only have 3 quarters. Dimes: 5 dimes can be combined with 2 quarters to make an even dollar. However, 4 dimes cannot be combined with the quarters that you already have to make a dollar, so you have 4 dimes. Nickels: Just one nickel can be combined with 2 dimes and 3 quarters. So you can't have any nickels. Pennies: 5 pennies is the same as one nickel, so you know you can't have that many. 4 pennies cannot be combined with any of your other coins to make a dollar. The final answer is: 3 quarters, 4 dimes, and 4 pennies.

FOOD FOR THE BRAIN ANSWERS

Lesson 18 - Flowering Plant Life Cycle - 180

Lesson 19 - Plant Parts & Function - fertilization, photosynthesis, germinate, leaves

Lesson 20 - Pollination - I have three flowers in my bouquet - one rose, one tulip, and one daisy

Lesson 21 - Birds - There were two little girl birds and a boy bird, their parents, and their father's parents, totaling 7 birds.

Lesson 22 - Bees - First he will fill the 5-gallon container. He will pour from the 5-gallon container into the 3-gallon one until it's full. The 5-gallon container now has 2 gallons left. He will then pour all the honey from the 3-gallon container back to the 8-gallon container, which will now have 6 gallons total. He will then pour the remaining 2 gallons from the 5-gallon container into the 3-gallon container, leaving just one gallon of space left. He will then fill the 5-gallon container again. He will then pour enough honey from the 5-gallon container to fill the 3-gallon container that already has 2 gallons. He will then have 4 gallons left in the 5-gallon container.

Lesson 23 - Butterflies - 200 days (365 days + (33 weeks x 7 days = 231) 231 days + 4 days = 600 / 3 = 200 days)

Lesson 24 - Snails - The snail travels at night because it is nocturnal. On the first evening, the snail climbs up 9 feet and slips down 6 feet while sleeping. So the next morning it is 3 feet from where it started (oy!). Therefore the snail travels 3 feet up the wall every day. Therefore, in 17 days, it has traveled a distance of 51 feet from the bottom. On the last day, the snail travels 9 feet upwards and reaches the top of the wall in a total of 18 days.

Lesson 25 - Worms

4	3	8
9	5	1
2	7	6

Lesson 26 - Garden Pests - Snail, beetle, aphid, caterpillar, moth

Lesson 27 - Spores & Fungi - fun, fig, fin, fug

Lesson 28 - Harvest Time & Preserving Food - **3 pancakes.** She would start by cooking two pancakes, and after 3 minutes, flip one over and remove the other from the pan half cooked and set it aside (3 minutes elapsed). Then she would add another pancake to the pan and after 3 minutes the first pancake would be done and the new pancake half done (6 minutes elapsed). She would flip the new pancake over to finish being cooked and add the pancake that was set aside half cooked and finish cooking that one as well (9 minutes elapsed).

Lesson 29 - Types of Plants - Mila has five gnomes and Mischa has seven gnomes.

Lesson 30 - Fruit & Vegetable Nutrition - The old cherry tree is 40, and the new cherry tree is 10.

Lesson 31 - Food Geography - The big monkey rows a small monkey over; the big monkey comes back. The big monkey rows the other small monkey over; the big monkey comes back. Two humans row over; a human and a small monkey come back. (Now two humans, the big monkey, and a small monkey are on the starting side of the river, and the third human and the second small monkey are on the destination side.) human and the big monkey row over; the human and a small monkey come back. Two humans row over; the big monkey rows back. (Now all the monkeys are on the starting side of the river, and all the humans are on the destination side.) The big monkey rows a small monkey over; the big monkey comes back. Then the big monkey rows the other small monkey over.

Lesson 32 - GMO: Genetically Modified Organisms - 50%

NOTE

While this workbook works great for kids grades 2 through 6 in a classroom environment, it works equally well for homeschoolers or parents who want to expose their children to the world of gardening and plant science at home.

There are 32 lessons in total. You may want to start using this workbook in August or September for fall and winter gardens or wait until February or March for spring and summer gardens. If you start in February or March, you may want to do lessons twice a week so you can cover all 32 lessons before the end of the typical school year. If you choose this option, you may want to have the students pick just one project per week.

Although lesson days may be only 1 or 2 days per week, students should still water their plants daily. Used milk, juice or soda jugs make great watering cans.

Lessons build on each other. They are sequential and should be completed in order.

Unlike general handouts that get disposed of, stashed away, or lost from week to week, giving each child one of these workbooks can provide them with an opportunity to take home "their" book each week (and after the school year has ended) to read and reflect on lessons over and over again. Children will be inspired to maintain their gardens as well as create fun, inexpensive (or no cost) crafts during the summer months when school isn't in session.

In this workbook, we suggest using containers for gardens because they are low in cost, moveable, and can be personalized. In addition, with containers, each child can take them home at the end of the school year to keep gardening as part of their everyday life. Ask any nursery or gardening store if they can spare some containers or call a popular local landscaping company to see if they can save some for you from their next job. Searching on craigslist or posting an ad is also another way to ask for people's used plant containers.

If you want children to grow pineapple plants, ask your local grocery store's produce manager to save the tops of pineapples so the kids can plant them in a container. Despite the fact that they can take a few years to bear fruit, they are easy to grow and maintain.

Suggest to kids to save the seeds from the food they eat at home – no need to run to the garden nursery to buy expensive seeds. Reinforce the idea that gardening is an easy, inexpensive way to add some excitement to summer months when school is out and any seed is worth the time and energy to try and make it grow into a plant.

Lesson projects are detailed in the back of the book. A handful of projects require prep work the day or week before so please read the project notes each week.

Rulers, permanent markers of various colors, paint brushes, colored pencils, crayons, glue, hot glue, and scissors are some of the basic supplies that will always be used for craft projects from week to week. You may want ask parents/caregivers to sign-up to provide materials for the each lesson's project to keep everybody contributing and involved. At the very least, encourage families to save milk/juice jugs, wine corks, opened food cans, kraft paper from shipping boxes, cereal boxes and toilet paper rolls for projects!

Comments regarding this workbook are welcome on the workbook's website – please share your experiences or provide tips with projects, lesson ideas, book suggestions, or anything else relevant to making this workbook a success for all teachers and students using it. Links to inexpensive craft supplies as well as additional information and resources are also listed on the workbook's website. **http://www.christahastie.com/gardeningworkbook**

The back page of each lesson page provides a space for children to write per the lesson's creative writing prompt as well as space to take measurements, sketch their plants and jot notes on their plant's progress from week to week. Encourage kids to use additional paper if necessary for their writing and for figuring out math problems. You may also want to consider taking photos of each child's workbook sketches from lesson to lesson, and making a cool flipbook for each child at the end of the year.

You may want to display completed projects each week, then stockpile them (not the crafts involving live plants, obviously). At the end of the school year, you can then give children a beautiful box full of their handcrafted goodies to take home. This way they can experience the excitement of seeing their creations all over again by unwrapping their boxes at home and placing some of their crafts in their container gardens that they also took home. You might also suggest that they can save some of the crafty projects for upcoming birthdays or holiday gift giving as many of these crafts make lovely gifts.

There is a graph template at the beginning of the workbook so kids can plot their recorded plant height measurements for their two selected plants from week to week after completing each lesson.

A suggested approach to teaching in the classroom environment can be found on the back of this page.

Allocate 1-1.5 hours of classroom time for each lesson:

- Have children take turns reading from the lesson page aloud

- Read the books of the week (or applicable excerpts from the books) as a class to continue learning about the lesson's topic

- Measurements & Observations: Have kids sketch and record their measurements and observations for their plants on the back of the lesson page:
  - Sketch plants
  - Take measurements of growth and plot data on graph in the back of the workbook
  - Calculate plant harvest days remaining
  - Note any interesting observations
  - Take photos of each plants (optional)

- Project: Complete the project for the lesson

- Have children water and maintain their seed cups / container gardens!

- Creative Writing Sharing: Have children share their creative writing pieces from the previous lesson

Post-Lesson Homework

- Creative Writing: Have children write 1-2 paragraphs on the back of each lesson page based on the lesson's creative writing prompt

- Gardening Dictionary: Have children create gardening dictionary flashcards on blank index cards for each lesson by writing the vocabulary word along with an illustration depicting the word on one side, and the definition on back

PROJECT

Lesson 1 - Planning For a Year-Round Garden / Personal Garden Planning

Have kids fill out the garden planning page in the front of the workbook based on the seeds or plants they would like to have in their own gardens. You may want to have some of the books listed in Lesson 4 available so kids can select from regrown plants such as potatoes, sweet potatoes, onions, and celery in addition to selecting plants to grow from seed by having a variety of seed packets laid out on classroom tables. This way kids can make their own decisions on what plants they would like to grow in their individual container gardens. They can then fill out their calendars based on the seeds and regrown plants selected. The completed calendars will serve as a guide for Lesson 2 when they start their seeds and regrown plants.

Supplies: Variety of seed packets, books from Lesson 4

Lesson 2 - Planting Seeds - Germination / Starting Seeds   ADVANCE PREP NEEDED

Yay! The seeds must get started this week so we can kick start the gardening fun! Use 8-10 clear cups per child with holes poked through the bottom (use a sharp needle - heat the needle if necessary) for a few drainage holes. Some good soil, a variety of seeds, and prepared regrown plants are all you need to get this project done. You may need to prepare up to a week in advance if kids have planned to use regeneration methods to grow some of their plants such as potatoes and sweet potatoes (refer to some of the books listed in Lesson 4 as a guide). Use a permanent marker to mark each child's name and the types of seeds planted in each cup on the front of each cup.

Supplies: Plastic clear cups (5 or 8 oz cups work great), permanent markers, various seeds, decent planting soil, liquid droppers (optional, for watering), books from Lesson 4

Lesson 3 - Container Gardening / Burlap Covered & Painted Plant Pots   ADVANCE PREP NEEDED

Measure the height and circumference of your plant containers. Cut rectangles of burlap measuring the 8-10" more than height of your planter and 6-8" wider than your measured circumference. You may want to do this a day or two before working with the kids depending on how many pots need wrapping. Two 5-gallon buckets or plant pots per child will work great. Wrap the fabric around the container and tuck the remaining fabric inside the pot. Add twine or burlap ribbon in the middle to keep the fabric in place. Have the kids paint the burlap for additional design charm. Seedlings will be planted in these lovely pots in a few weeks!

Website For Project Instructions: http://downtoearthstyle.blogspot.com/2012/04/bucket-burlap.html
Supplies: 5-gallon planter pots or buckets, burlap, twine or burlap ribbon, paint and paint brushes (optional)
Project/Image Credit: Thank you Holly, from the down to earth style blog (downtoearthstyle.blogspot.com)!

Lesson 4 - Regeneration: Regrown Gardening / Paint Stick Plant Markers   ADVANCE PREP NEEDED

You can smile at your local hardware store's paint specialists and ask for a handful or two of these great wooden paint stirrer sticks for free, especially if you're buying some paint. You can also order 100 of them for $13 on Amazon.com. Prepare for this project the day before by painting the sticks with white or colored base paint (you can get small sample size jars in any color at most major hardware stores) so they will be ready to personalize on project day! Kids can then draw or paint the plant names and illustrate the fruits or vegetables on each stick. It's also good idea to have kids write their name on the back of each of their markers.

Website For Project Instructions: http://www.repeatcrafterme.com/2013/04/paint-mixing-stick-garden-signs.html
Supplies: Paint stick stirrers, white paint, paint brush, colored permanent markers
Project/Image Credit: Thank you Sarah, from repeatcrafterme.com!

Lesson 5 - Garden Maintenance / Plant Seedlings in Pots Outside

Have kids add soil to their containers and dig 2-4 holes the size of their seedling containers per 5-gallon container. Kids can then carefully transplant their seedlings from their clear plastic cups into their containers, and add their paint stick markers carefully. Each child should also save 2 seedling cups for next week's project!

Supplies: Good vegetable garden soil

Lesson 6 - Gardening Benefits / Toilet Paper Roll Seedling Gifts

This project allows kids to have the pleasure of creating and giving a few simple gifts while also giving the recipient an opportunity to enjoy the benefits of gardening. Carolyn at carolynshomework.com details how simple this project is with a few basic supplies. The kraft paper used to wrap the TP rolls can be found stuffed inside boxes shipped to your home, so be on the lookout. Otherwise, it can be bought inexpensively online from amazon.com or other online retailers.

Website For Project Instructions: http://www.carolynshomework.com/2014/05/the-dirt-brown-paper-seedling-pots.html
Supplies: Seedlings, soil, toilet paper rolls, twine, Kraft paper
Project/Image Credit: Thank you Carolyn, from carolynshomework.com!

Lesson 7 - Garden Safety / Mini Garden Safety Warning Signs   ADVANCE PREP NEEDED

These signs are easy and inexpensive to create using small craft wood slats (Loew Cornell makes these in various sizes in packs of 6-12 for a few bucks on amazon.com) and can be placed inside each student's plant containers along with their plant markers to remind them of garden safety. Let students choose one or two signs to design and create based on the lesson and have them place the signs in their containers. You will want to prep the wooden boards by giving them a white base coat and hot gluing wooden coffee stirrer sticks to the back. Kids can then sketch their designs first on paper and use pencils to draw these designs on their wooden boards before they use paint or permanent markers to finalize their design in color.

Supplies: Small craft wood boards, wooden coffee stirrer sticks, white paint, paint/permanent markers, hot glue

Lesson 8 - Garden Tools / Shrinky Dink Garden Magnets

Have kids trace and color the various fruits, vegetables and garden tools found on the patterns page in the back of the workbook onto the shrinky dink paper. Cut, color, and pop them in the shrinky dink machine and boom!!! -- Shrinky Dink magic!
Glue craft magnet circles on the back and this project is a wrap!

Website For Project Instructions: http://blog.crescendoh.com/gallery/2012/02/stamped-mason-jar-shrinky-dink-pendants-tutorial-by-shona-cole.html
Supplies: Shrinky dink machine (if you don't have one, many thrift stores have them for a few bucks or you can buy new online at amazon.com or other online retailers), shrinky dink paper, markers, glue, craft magnet circles
Project/Image Credit: Thank you Shona, author of The Artistic Mother (http://amzn.to/1V0Tsf6)

Lesson 9 - Healthy Soil & Mulch / Leaf Art Cards

Leaves can be transformed into amazing cards that kids to give to their family and friends. A fun scavenger hunt around the schoolyard for various fallen, dried leaves will provide the bulk of materials and inspiration for this project. Ask the kids to plan their designs first by laying out the leaves from their hunt. Then they can recreate their design on cardstock and add eyes with Sharpies for a quick, fun and creative project. See Ksu's tutorial for more information and inspiration at kokokoKIDS.ru. There are also several neat books that showcase leaf art that may be fun to have kids look at for inspiration such as Look What I Did With A Leaf! by Morteza E. Sohi.

Website For Project Instructions: http://www.kokokokids.ru/2011/09/fall-leaves-craft-ideas.html
Supplies: Leaves, cardstock, glue, permanent markers
Project/Image Credit: Thank you Ksu, from www.kokokokids.ru!

Lesson 10 - Compost / Compost Collection & Awareness Posters

Using simple small poster boards, ask kids to plan and design a compost awareness poster: what is compost, and what ingredients are good and bad for compost. They can even attach gallon sized plastic Ziploc bags to solicit student donations for the class compost bin by placing the posters around the schoolyard. Then create a simple, small class compost bin by following the instructions on the lesson page and have kids dump their "donations" as they become available.

Supplies: Poster boards, gallon size sealable bags, markers/crayons
Project/Image Credit: Thank you to artist Joe Wirtheim for your inspiring compost art (victorygardenoftomorrow.com)!

Lesson 11 - Ecosystems / Mini Terrarium Ecosystems

Little terrariums house mini ecosystems that are whimsical and magical for both adults and kids alike, plus they are so easy and fun to make. Clear plastic globes or bowls are easy to find online or at dollar stores. Succulent plants and moss are found at nurseries and even some grocery stores. Have kids look for small pebbles or stones to add to their terrarium. And for added extra charm, allow each child to pick 1-2 plastic figurines to add an interesting element to the terrarium. Various mini plastic figurines can be also found at thrift stores, dollar stores or from a variety of retailers online.

Website For Project Instructions: http://diyready.com/easy-diy-projects-how-to-make-succulent-diy-terrarium/
Supplies: Clear jars/bowls/boxes, succulents, moss, rocks, soil, glue, plastic figurines

Lesson 12 - Biodiversity / Paper Mâché Globes

With some basic inexpensive supplies, these paper mâché earth globes make such a fun project. Plus kids can gently poke holes with a toothpick when they're dry and add a battery operated LED tealight candle or string lights (found on craft sites and amazon.com) inside to turn these globes into beautiful nightlights.

Website For Project Instructions: http://www.lowes.com/creative-ideas/woodworking-and-crafts/papier-mache-earth/project
Supplies: Balloons, flour, newspaper, green and blue tissue paper, disposable cups/plates, toothpicks, battery operated tealight candles or string lights (optional)
Project/Image Credit: Thank you, Lowes.com!

PROJECT

This simple and inexpensive craft lures all the pretty birds in the neighborhood to your garden to help create a thriving ecosystem. Just spread peanut butter on a TP roll, cover with bird seeds, and add some pretty ribbon so it can be hung from a tree.

Website For Project Instructions: http://diyready.com/crafts-for-kids-toilet-paper-roll-craft-projects/
Supplies: Toilet paper rolls, seeds, peanut butter, ribbon
Project/Image Credit: Thank you to DIYready.com!

Have kids cut around the outline of the sun art template from the back of the workbook. Using natural materials outside like crushed leaves, flower petals and dirt, have kids paste the materials on the page to create a mixed media piece of art. For example, the sun rays may use crumbled yellow leaves while the background sky may use dirt. You can also add bowls of rice, small beans, and other random things that would otherwise be trash (for example, plastic cups cut up into tiny pieces) to add splashes of color and texture to the art piece.

Supplies: Glue, natural materials, clean "trash"

Who eats who? Have an array of food chain books (The A Who-Eats-What Adventure series and Who Eats What? Food Chains and Food Webs series are great for kids) available for kids to peruse and learn about who eats who in various food chains. When they have it figured out, they can cut images of animals, plants and decomposers involved in these food chains around the world from the back of the workbook. Alternatively challenge kids to draw their own animals, plants and decomposers in the food chain they selected. The cut or drawn images can then be pasted on cardstock blank bookmarks to show who eats who. Blank cardstock bookmarks are inexpensive and can be bought online from a number of online retailers. Add a ribbon or have kids bead a tassel at the top for an extra cool touch.

Supplies: Blank cardstock bookmarks (or make your own from cutting cardstock sheets), markers, ribbon/string/beads (optional)

ADVANCE PREP NEEDED
Mandalas are a spiritual and ritual symbol in many religions that represent the universe, wholeness, wisdom and compassion. And rocks make the perfect platform for kids to create their own mandalas. You will want to prepare a few days before by cleaning the rocks and when dry, painting them with black or white acrylic craft paint for the base coat. Then have kids follow Barbara's simple instructions at colorful-crafts.com to create these beautiful mandalas as decorations in their gardens with permanent markers or paint.

Website For Project Instructions: http://www.listotic.com/29-fun-crafts-kids-adults-will-actually-enjoy/3/
Supplies: Rocks, paint, permanent markers
Project/Image Credit: Thank you Barbara, from colorful-crafts.com!

Seed collection books are so neat and cool, inspiring kids to save seeds to hopefully be planted one day! Using some small white coin envelopes, some recycled cardboard and some glue, kids can create an envelope book to store seeds quickly and easily thanks to the TwoCraftingSisters tutorial. To make it easy, templates from the TwoCraftingSisters tutorial are available in the back of the workbook for kids to cut and trace onto cardboard and cardstock per the instructions. And to be extra earth friendly, use cardboard food boxes (cereal, couscous boxes) in lieu of buying chipboard.

Website For Project Instructions: http://craftylifeandstyle.blogspot.com/2011/03/guest-blog-mini-book-made-fron-scratch.html
Supplies: White coin envelopes (4-10 per student), glue, pretty cardstock paper, cardboard boxes
Project/Image Credit: Thank you Maura and Sheila, from twocraftingsisters.blogspot.com!

ADVANCE PREP NEEDED
To prepare, dry various flowers and leaves by placing them inside the pages of big, heavy books 3-7 days before doing this craft with kids so they can flatten. Dried leaf and flower bookmarks are easy, fun and beautiful. Simply take dried flowers and leaves and have kids glue them on blank cardstock bookmarks or use one of DIYready.com's wax paper and iron tricks. You can also add a colorful ribbon at the top to give an extra colorful touch.

Website For Project Instructions: http://diyready.com/how-to-press-flowers/
Supplies: Dried flowers and leaves, cardstock bookmarks, Mod Podge (or glue), ribbon/beads (optional), wax paper/iron (optional)
Project/Image Credit: Thank you to DIYready.com!

PROJECT DETAILS FOR EACH LESSON

Lesson 19 - Plant Parts & Function / Tree of Life With Notes & Quotes

The "Tree of Life" concept stems from trees having been considered powerful symbols of growth, death and rebirth around the world throughout the ages. This simple art piece is a powerful craft that uses dead branches to house little "ornaments" of paper with inspirational quotes and nice notes written by classmates. Have kids find nice dead branches around the school yard, and have them paint or glue and glitter them. They can then fill small plastic bowls with cement and stick their branch inside. They may also want to stick some craft moss and/or glass pebbles on the cement for an added decorative touch before the cement dries. While the bowls and branches are drying, have a variety of inspirational quote books available so kids can copy their favorites on small pieces of paper and hang from their trees with ribbon, yarn or string. You can also ask classmates to write a positive note to each fellow classmate as a unique homework assignment. Each of the special notes can then be exchanged and hung from the tree the following day. These trees can be amazingly inspirational for kids.

Supplies: Dead branches, glitter, glue, paint, paint brushes, cement, bucket for mixing cement, plastic bowls, small pieces of paper, ribbon/yarn/string, craft moss and glass stones (optional)

Lesson 20 - Pollination / Paper Flowers

Colorful cardstock, hot glue, and skewers are all you need to create a beautiful floral bouquet. Add glitter and leaves for the extra touch. Have kids make one flower or an entire bouquet wrapped with ribbon.

Website For Project Instructions: http://onelittleproject.com/how-to-make-rolled-paper-flowers/
Supplies: Colorful cardstock, hot glue, skewers/coffee stirrers
Project/Image Credit: Thank you Debbie, from onelittleproject.com!

Lesson 21 - Birds / Felt Circle & Ribbon Birds   ADVANCE PREP NEEDED

Kids love these felt circle birds because they're colorful, easy to make and special little keepsakes. The 3" diameter felt circles are a great size for small birds and can be bought from amazon in bags of 100 in various colors. You may want to hot glue a 2" or 1.5" felt circle in the middle of the 3" circles in a different color or have the kids sew it on before the rest of the bird is sewn for an extra colorful bird. Fold the felt circle in half and pin 3-4 loops of ribbon to the back, with 1" of ribbon inside the bird. Pin a small triangle on the front for the beak, with some of the beak remaining inside the bird. Sew half of the bird together along the edge, then stuff with polyfil. Finish sewing the bird all the way, and sew on or glue on 3-4mm black beads or googly eyes on each side for eyes.

Website For Project Instructions: http://winkdesigns.typepad.com/wink_designs/2011/12/ribbon-birds.html
Supplies: 3" and 1.5" felt circles, yellow felt sheet, thread, needles, ribbon, polyfil, 3mm black beads
Project/Image Credit: Thank you Marina, from Peach Patterns (www.winkdesigns.typepad.com)!

Lesson 22 - Bees / Upcycled Wine Cork Pendants   ADVANCE PREP NEEDED

Ask your local bar to save wine corks for you for this project - one per child will work great. Have an adult cut 3-4 discs from each natural cork with a sharp knife or razor blade. You may want to add a base paint coat before you have kids decorate them with stamps, permanent markers, glitter, or paint. To make pendants, screw in 5mm silver jewelry screw eyes to the top, and add necklace cord. For magnets, simply glue craft magnet pieces to the back.

Website For Project Instructions: http://www2.fiskars.com/Ideas-and-How-Tos/Crafting-and-Sewing/Upcycling/Upcycled-Wine-Cork-Pendants#.UfqssKwpjw1
Supplies: Wine corks, permanent markers, paint, stamps, glitter, glue, 5mm silver screw eyes for jewelry, craft magnet pieces
Project/Image Credit: Thank you, fiskars.com!

Lesson 23 - Butterflies / Artist Trading Cards

Artist Trading Cards are a fun, miniature work of art that are meant to be traded, shared and swapped with friends and other artists. Using 2 1/2" x 3 1/2" blank cardstock, kids should create 6-8 identical ATCs using any material and design they like on the front and with the artist's name on the back of the card (traditionally contact information would also be on the back). They can then trade, share and swap with classmates when they are dry.

Website For Project Instructions: http://blog.consumercrafts.com/paper-crafts/about-atcs-artist-trading-cards/
Supplies: 2 1/2" x 3 1/2" blank cardstock cards, various materials and stamps, glue
Project/Image Credit: Thank you, consumercrafts.com!

PROJECT

Lesson 24 - Snails / Polymer Clay Snail Decorations

BlackBetty's LAB has a wonderful step-by-step photo tutorial on how to create these cute little snails using polymer clay, seed beads and craft flower pistils. If you can, bake the snails for 15 minutes at 200 degrees. A simple toaster oven will do the trick. When cooled, coat them with Sculpey Glaze ($2) to make the snails appear more rich, deep, and colorful. They will make great additions to any gardens!

Website For Project Instructions: http://blackbettyslab.blogspot.com/search/label/animali
Supplies: Polymer clay, craft flower pistils, black seed beads, Sculpey Glaze
Project/Image Credit: Thank you Elizabeth, from BlackBetty's LAB (blackbettyslab.blogspot.it)!

Lesson 25 - Worms / Wool Bookworm Bookmarks

These adorable worm bookmarks are the original creation of artist Belinda Leidel in Germany. While these one-of-a-kind worms can be bought from her online store, have kids give worm bookmark making a try. Use Angola mohair cashmere wool knitting yarn because it can be "brushed", making them fun and funky worms. Use Styrofoam fill balls (open up a bean bag and grab a handful :)!!) and hot glue them on to the area that was just wrapped with the body colored yarn. Then use a black permanent marker to finish the eyes.

Supplies: 2 colors of Angola mohair cashmere wool knitting yarn, Styrofoam white fill balls, black marker, fine comb
Project/Image Credit: Thank you, Belinda Leidel (https://www.etsy.com/shop/Lescatole)!

Lesson 26 - Garden Pests / Circle of Life Plant Flipbook

Flipbooks are just so cool and fun. By flipping pages, an animated story plays through images. Have kids cut, color and order each of the pictures from the page in the back of this workbook depicting the circle of life for a plant...including pests! Then have them glue the colored pictures on 3 x 2.5 mini half index cards (flip books work better with thicker paper). Add blank mini index cards for the front cover and back of the book and then follow Brit + Co's simple instructions on how to finish creating the book with just tape and glue. Challenge kids to design the book's cover and come up with a nifty title for the book.

Website For Project Instructions: http://www.brit.co/diy-flipbook/
Supplies: 3 x 2.5 mini half index cards, glue, packing tape, markers, small binder clips
Project/Image Credit: Thank you Brit + Co (www.brit.co)!

Lesson 27 - Spores & Fungi / Mini Polymer Clay Mushrooms

These little polymer clay mushrooms are so cute and easy to make. Have kids make a few mushrooms each with straight pins and polymer clay as shown in the video on the PixieHill blog. Then if you like, fill some thimbles half way with hot glue, stuff in craft moss and quickly place the mushrooms for a cute, whimsical mushroom thimble garden.

Website For Project Instructions: http://blog.pixiehill.com/2012/02/how-to-make-teeny-weeny-mushrooms.html
Supplies: Thimbles, craft moss, red and white polymer clay, straight pins, hot glue

Lesson 28 - Harvest Time & Preserving Food / Strawberry Potpourri Sachets

These little strawberries are quick and easy to create and make any room or clothing drawer smell nice and clean because of the potpourri inside them. I find that smaller potpourri pieces and gender neutral scents including cinnamon, citrus and vanilla work best when it comes to selecting a potpourri filler. The ginderella.com blog details the creation process.

Website For Project Instructions: http://www.ginderellas.com/2012/11/wool-strawberry-sachet.html
Supplies: Red felt, green felt, clear seed beads, thread, needles, potpourri
Project/Image Credit: Thank you Paula, from ginderella.com!

Lesson 29 - Types of Plants / Pinecone Gnomes

Pinecones are a great foundation for many craft projects including these cute little pinecone gnomes. With a few simple additional supplies, kids will be able to create these cute garden decorations in no time. The webloomhere blog details the creation process using smaller pinecones. If you have trouble finding pinecones, improvise by using acorns, nuts or other natural materials found in your neck of the woods :).

Website For Project Instructions: http://webloomhere.blogspot.com/2011/12/pinecone-gnomes.html
Supplies: Small pinecones, various felt shets, 1-inch wooden beads with 3/8th inch holes, thread, needles, colored pencils, hot glue
Project/Image Credit: Thank you Margaret, from webloomhere.blogspot.com!

PROJECT DETAILS FOR EACH LESSON

Lesson 30 - Fruit & Vegetable Nutrition / Paper Mâché Watermelon Bowl

This cute watermelon bowl is a fun project that can be made easily. If you're trying to get it done in one day, have kids flip a disposable bowl upside down and cover with plastic wrap. Paper mâché 2-3 layers with newspaper, then with tissue paper in various shades of green. Then cover the inside of another disposable bowl with plastic wrap and turn the paper mached bowl so it's right side up and place inside the clean, lined bowl. Remove the bowl and remove the plastic wrap slowly. You may need to place them in the sun or use a hairdryer for a few minutes if the paper mâché is too wet. Then paper mâché the inside of the bowl with dark pink or red tissue paper and let dry. When dry, remove plastic and use a black permanent marker to draw seeds inside the bowl.

Website For Project Instructions: http://handmadekidsart.com/fun-paper-crafts/#_a5y_p=1945480
Supplies: Newspaper, various shades of green tissue paper, red or pink tissue paper, flour/glue, disposable bowls, plastic wrap, black permanent marker
Project/Image Credit: Thank you Jaime, from handmadekidsart.com!

Lesson 31 - Food Geography / Who Grows What Where? Maps

This is a great project that could also be turned into a fun fieldtrip to your local grocery store in addition to a classroom activity. If you have the opportunity to take the class on a fieldtrip, ask the store manager ahead of time if they would be willing to let kids sample the various produce on display. Then allow the kids to play detective in the produce area by investigating labels and signs surrounding each fruit or vegetable. They should jot notes in a notebook about what is grown where. If you can't get to a grocery store, you can always borrow a variety of books from the library (see book list on the lesson page) and have kids research the information in the books to determine what is grown where. Then have them create labels with fruit and vegetable names and images and stick them on world maps with glue or double stick tape. Check out the kidworldcitizen.org blog for details and teaching points on this activity. Kids have fun learning about geography, food choices, environmental impacts, and nutrition.

Website For Project Instructions: http://kidworldcitizen.org/2012/08/24/where-in-the-world-is-your-food-from/
Supplies: World maps, paper, markers, glue
Project/Image Credit: Thank you Becky, from kidworldcitizen.org!

Lesson 32 - GMO: Genetically Modified Organisms / Mr. Recycle Head Planter   ADVANCE PREP NEEDED

This planter is so cute and whimsical and makes a fun addition to any room. The GMO concepts are loosely tied in because the planter is sort of a hodge podge of various elements all rolled into one fantastic wheatgrass planter. Check thrift stores and eBay for lots of Mr. Potato Head shoes - I was able to acquire 26 pairs of shoes for under $25. For the wheatgrass, you may want to grow some 2-3 days before. See the deliacreates.com website for detailed how-to instructions on this project.

Website For Project Instructions: http://www.deliacreates.com/mr-recycle-head-man/
Supplies: Tin cans, hammer, nail, felt scraps, pipe cleaners, Mr. Potato Head feet, hot glue, recycled cleaned plastic containers, googly eyes
Project/Image Credit: Thank you Delia, from deliacreates.com!

CPSIA information can be obtained
at www.ICGtesting.com
Printed in the USA
LVHW072245240822
726832LV00002B/11